Bobby Ba

Winning Poker Secrets

Bobby Baldwin's Winning Poker Secrets

Mike Caro

CARDOZA PUBLISHING

Cardoza Publishing is the foremost gaming publisher in
the world, with a library of over 100 up-to-date and easy-
to-read books and strategies. These authoritative works are
written by the top experts in their fields and, with more
than 7,000,000 books in print, represent the best-selling and
most popular gaming books anywhere.

SECOND EDITION

Copyright © 1979, 2004 by
B & G Publishing Co., Inc.
- All Rights Reserved -

This Cardoza edition is printed by special arrangement with
B & G Publishing Co., Inc.

Library of Congress Catalog Card No: 2004100552
ISBN: 1-58042-129-6

Visit our new web site (www.cardozapub.com)
or write us for a full list of Cardoza books,
advanced and computer strategies.

CARDOZA PUBLISHING
P.O. Box 1500, Cooper Station, New York, NY 10276
Phone (800)577-WINS
email: cardozapub@aol.com
www.cardozapub.com

ACKNOWLEDGEMENTS

(Alphabetically)

Benny Binion

Jack Binion

Doyle Brunson

Mike Caro

Jimmy "The Greek" Snyder

Bobby at the Poker Hall of Fame

To My Family

CONTENTS

Forewords

(today's and yesterday's)

By Doyle Brunson
(World Champion of Poker, 1976 & 1977)

BOBBY BALDWIN TODAY —
25 YEARS AFTER THE ADVENTURE

If you ask me, there has never been another poker story like Bobby Baldwin's. Get ready to accompany him from the pool halls in Tulsa to the poker world championship in Las Vegas. It is adventure stacked atop adventure. And it's all real. This book will lead you right up to the day Bobby established himself as world champion of poker twenty-five years ago—at the age of 27.

The whole adventure didn't end on the last page of this book —just the poker part. Bobby's success story continued beyond poker. After winning the seven-card stud and deuce-to-the seven championship events in 1977 at the World Series of Poker, held at Binion's Horseshoe, Bobby claimed the main-event world championship in 1978.

So, after proving himself as a world-class poker player, able to handle and humble the best in the world, Bobby shocked many of his fellow players. He showed that he could quickly become one of the truly legendary gaming executives. That didn't shock me, though. You've got to gauge what's inside a man to truly understand his potential. Bobby always had the potential for whatever he chose to do in life beyond poker.

No, it didn't surprise me when, in 1982, Bobby went to work for Steve Wynn at the Golden Nugget in Las Vegas. After a few months in the card room, he soared into management and then became president of the Golden Nugget in less than two years.

He continued his meteoric rise in the gaming industry when the Mirage opened in 1987, by becoming president of that casino—the most lavish in the history of Las Vegas. In fact, the Mirage set the stage for all the new super casino complexes that the city is famous for today. Yes, Bobby was there, right there, right in the center of the storm that would transform Las Vegas forever.

And it didn't stop there. When the $1.5 billion Bellagio opened in 1997, he chose to take his services there, becoming its first and only president. When MGM bought the Bellagio, some might have thought that would be the end of Bobby's career there. Well, not if you were a smart buyer. And Kirk Krikorian was a smart buyer. He retained Bobby, who is still active today as president of the Bellagio and CEO of Mirage Resorts, heading the most admired and talked-about gaming establishments in the world.

Bobby has lived a fast paced life, including off-road stock car racing, playing high stakes poker, and pursing his passion for golf.

Shirley, Bobby's first wife and the mother of his children, Staci and BJ, died from cancer in 1996. Bobby is married now to a former Miss Nevada beauty contest winner, Donna McNeil. He resides in Las Vegas with Donna and BJ. Staci lives with her husband and their two children in Los Angeles.

Bobby was interviewed for this book in 1979 by Mike Caro. There was no manuscript and the book possibly has historical note as the first ever written entirely on primitive computer typesetting equipment, in one run-through. I know, I bought that equipment and published the book.

Mike brought Bobby's story to life as a tribute to a fellow player, but wanted a chance to finally edit and perfect the text after all these years. The result is what you'll be reading today, blending the third-person narrative about Bobby's real-life adventures with first-person passages in Bobby's own words.

This book has been revised and republished because of the explosion of poker popularity that is rocking the world today—and because of the many requests that it be put back in print.

There's so much to say about Bobby's life that I almost forgot to mention: Bobby received the ultimate honor of being inducted into the Poker Hall of Fame in 2003.

ORIGINAL BRUNSON FOREWORD, 1979 – AN INTRODUCTION TO THE ADVENTURE

"Bobby won all the money again!"

The reports blew through the poker grapevine like a dry wind out of Texas. I mean, it was always the same thing, always the same story. Some kid had invaded the traveling pro poker circuit down Texas way and taken over where I'd left off. After having played twenty years in Texas, I was naturally curious.

Who was this kid who'd appeared out of nowhere to dominate the group of established poker professionals? Quite frankly, I was getting pretty irritated hearing about this Bobby. Just wait until I get this kid across the table from me! I thought.

Well, I finally got him across that table. First thing I knew, I was a forty thousand dollar loser trying to run over him. I finally settled down and got even, but Bobby won all the money. Again! I knew how Pat Garrett must have felt about Billy the Kid a hundred years ago.

After I got to know Bobby, it wasn't hard to understand how he'd mastered poker in such a short time. He approaches all poker games with such professional diligence and intensity that he absorbs the fine points almost immediately.

The longer I play with the Owl, the more I watch in amazement the subtle, intricate maneuvers and strategies he employs. They took me years to perfect.

The fact that Bobby is an all-round poker master was established in 1977 when he came to Binion's Horseshoe Club and walked away with the World Series of Poker titles in both Seven-Stud and Deuce-to-Seven Lowball. Those two conquests netted him $135,000. As you know he won the big event in 1978, the nationally televised no-limit Hold 'em championship at Binion's. That was worth $210,000. Bobby is a poker professional who doesn't care who's playing, what they're playing or how high the stakes are. When he approaches a poker table, his vocabulary seems to be limited to, "Deal me in."

He's so super-aggressive that I sometimes wonder why he doesn't get a sore arm from shoving all his chips to the center of the table so often. Despite his aggressive brand of poker, Bobby's one of the most pleasant and gracious persons I've ever known . . . a true Southern gentleman.

He prefers the life of a traveling poker player, going wherever the action happens to be. Since he's only a phone call away, he "mysteriously" shows up whenever there's a no-limit game or when they're playing $1,000-limit Hold 'em.

Being on the road constantly is a tough life—I can tell you from experience. But chasing that white line down the middle of the highway is exciting and rewarding if, like Bobby, you're talented enough to make it happen.

Bobby Baldwin (center) and Doyle Brunson (right)

INTRODUCTION

Find out what it takes to be a pro through this intimate look at one of the best players in the world. An enthralling combination of advice and anecdote, *Bobby Baldwin's Winning Poker Secrets* is the story of how a young man from Tulsa became a world champion poker player. Watch Bobby climb his way to the top in an amazing story full of bad beats, big wins, excitement, and insight.

What does it take? Observe the winning characteristics of a professional poker player. Find out how, in his own words, Bobby Baldwin became a World Series of Poker champion, a world-class poker player, and one of the most influential people in Las Vegas. This book is a poker classic, along with *According to Doyle*, now titled *Poker Wisdom of a Champion*.

Bobby is now a driving force in Vegas as the President and CEO of MGM's Bellagio Casino. He continues to play high-limit poker with the greatest players in the world.

Bobby Baldwin is a gambler who grew up. Some don't. A lot die broke and begging, chasing a grade school fantasy beyond their sixties, still believing that luck—the god of Luck who shoveled them under—will dig them out as a last loving gesture.

Bobby Baldwin, the poker champion of the world at twenty-seven, grew up after too much pain. He didn't suddenly wake up Christmas morning with the wisdom required to demolish poker opponents. Wisdom grew day by day over fifteen years of mistakes and suffering.

There never lived a poker player who got smart overnight. There are too many traps hidden along the path to the World Series of Poker. Even for Bobby, blessed with his keen mind and perceptive outlook, the struggle was long.

Taking Chances

We have self-destructive urges. All of us. And to deny this is to summon financial disaster. In the competitive world of professional poker, no one learns easily. But if we never confront our own natures, then we never learn at all.

"The first thing you've got to understand," Bobby says softly, "is that there's nothing wrong, nothing sinful, nothing insane about taking reckless chances. Anyone who ever made an invention, fought for justice or climbed a mountain, took a chance. The people who risked security the most, the ones who put their stability or their bankrolls on the line—those are the great ones sparkling from cover to cover throughout every history book." He looks earnest. He is earnest. He stares directly into your eyes and speaks in a soothing mid-western tone. You feel comfortable.

When certain that you comprehend his meaning, he smiles and continues. "I've known many gamblers to bet whole bankrolls in a single pot. And that's not a bad quality. It's something to be admired. Takes raw courage. But as the years passed, certain things began to sink in with me. There are methods to keep from getting broke— ways to stay in the money and climb the highest mountain without leaning over the ledge so far that the risk is intolerable. There's pain associated with getting broke. I've felt it enough times. When this book about Bobby Baldwin comes out, it's got to deal truthfully with gambling urges and why most good players fail to acquire a lasting bankroll. Maybe my years of pain and learning will save the readers a lot of agony."

Mistakes to Avoid

"And I want to supply the readers with a list of the most common mistakes the average player makes in all the most popular poker games, Seven-Stud, Hold 'em, and Five-Card Draw. I want to discuss these mistakes and show how to avoid them. But most of all, I'd like my book to take the reader on tour with me. After all, I'm a traveling poker professional. We'll go from game to game focusing on my mistakes and my successes. That's the sort of honest, direct approach to teaching poker that no other book has ever taken."

Bobby Baldwin (Photo by Ulvis Alberts.)

CHAPTER 1

The End of the Road

BINION'S HORSESHOE CLUB
LAS VEGAS (MAY 19, 1978)

The television cameras are gone from the poker tables. Most of the players and reporters have crowded into the Sombrero Room, the Horseshoe Club's popular Mexican restaurant. Some stand by the swinging doors and gaze back across two rows of blackjack tables to where the poker combat ended half an hour earlier. It seems lonely over there, even with technicians noisily gathering their equipment while several non-tournament poker games continue.

Across the casino, the excitement has ended. Bobby Baldwin, known to his admirers as "the Owl," has just claimed the 1978 World Series of Poker main event, defeating forty-one other players—including the best professionals from around the country. He's earned $210,000 first prize money, half of the $420,000 awarded to the top five finishers. On this side of the Horseshoe Club, there's a celebration in the restaurant, full of laughter and congratulations.

So many questions are forced on Bobby from friends and reporters that few coherent words are registered. Voice competes with anonymous voice. Fragmented sentences cut short and forgotten. Bobby smiles, tries to answer, but he's overwhelmed by the rapidity of the questioning.

Her eyes pretty and sparkling, his wife Shirley sits beside him. Sipping coffee, she pretends to listen to the muddled questions and chirped kudos. But you suspect that her thoughts and Bobby's are afloat elsewhere. Thinking how sweet this ultimate poker success

21

really is. Remembering the good times and the hard times along the road. All mingle and blur—good breaks and bad beats.

Questions. Relentless questions. "Where were you born?" "I wanted to ask if—" "Let me find this out first, do you—" "How does it feel?" "What makes you so much better than the rest?"

Doyle Brunson and "Amarillo Slim" Preston return to the table. Earlier they'd slipped away through a crowd of reporters, escaping scarcely noticed. Doyle, famous in poker circles as "Texas Dolly," won the world title in both 1976 and 1977. Slim also claimed the championship previously.

Doyle opens his broad hand and smiles warmly. Like Bobby, he's an even-tempered man you immediately admire. Forty-five and corpulent, he was once an All-American basketball player and track star. In the palm of his hand is a pack of $100 bills secured by a rubber band. Dolly casts an affectionate and fatherly glance toward Bobby. The usually animated Slim sits smiling and tips his expensive cowboy hat. Ostentatiously, Dolly begins counting through the wad.

The questions from acquaintances and reporters—some passing by and some hovering ungraciously around the table—taper off. Everyone watches as Dolly continues counting money. Toward the end of the pile, he snaps the bills crisply and chants, "Twenty-nine thousand eight hundred, twenty-nine thousand nine hundred, thirty thousand. Thanks, Bobby. It took a lot of trouble, but I finally found some goose silly enough to bet against you."

More congratulations. Puggy Pearson leans across Shirley's shoulder to shake Bobby's hand. Puggy's arrival means there are now four world poker champions present. Sensing opportunity, several photographers flash their cameras. Jack Binion walks by, slaps Bobby on the back and politely promises to return shortly. Seems some high-roller wants the limit raised on the crap table, and Jack is eager to oblige.

Shirley rewards Bobby with a hug, while—quietly beneath the table—she grabs his hand and squeezes tight. Then, more questions from news writers.

"How long have you been playing poker?"

"Well, the first time was when I was twelve."

"Did you win?"

Bobby smiles, and his eyes radiate a magnetic honesty as he shakes his head. "No . . . no, I lost six dollars."

CHAPTER 2

Bobby's Poker Debut

MARK'S HOUSE
TULSA, OKLAHOMA

It's 1963 and Bobby has never gambled. Never pitched pennies or risked a quarter on a football game. Never shot marbles for money. Nothing.

Now the phone rings and it's Mark, one of his best friends—a classmate at his junior high school. Twelve-year-old Bobby has just ridden his bike home from school. He's sipping a Coke, daydreaming out the window, perhaps seeing an imaginary jungle in place of his front lawn and, no doubt, pretending to march into it gallantly.

He snatches the phone. Mark wants him to peddle right over and play poker. Poker? He hardly knows anything about it.

"We're not playing for much money," Mark assures him. "Whoever gets lucky is gonna win."

"I've got about six bucks," says Bobby, hoping the sum will impress Mark. Not every twelve year old carries six dollars in his pocket.

"That's plenty! Steve's over here with three-fifty, and Charlie says he ain't gonna lose no more than five."

"I never played before."

"It's just luck, like flipping a coin or something. We'll teach you."

"Okay. See you in a couple minutes."

Bobby peddled fast. He held no preconceptions about gambling. Nothing in the back of his conscience told him not to do it. Nothing drew him compulsively onward. No taboos, no encouragement. Yet, there it was—a spinning anticipation of adventure like he'd never felt before.

He laid his bike down softly on Mark's front lawn. It was an upper middle-class neighborhood with the yards manicured and the houses maintained. Bobby entered through the unlocked screen door. The living room was the site of a friendly argument.

Mark's voice. "That's crazy. A team never won no six pennants in a row!"

"Well, the Yankees done it twice." An unfamiliar voice.

Besides Mark, there were three others in the living room. These three went to a junior high in a different district, and Bobby knew none of them.

Mark's introduction was, "This is Bobby: Charlie, Steve, Tom." He didn't bother to say which was which.

It would be a five-handed game, and Mark took a deck of Hoyle cards from a cupboard while the rest seated themselves at the kitchen table. It wasn't an ideal playing surface. Not even a tablecloth—and that meant the cards would be hard to deal and to pick up. None of these five knew any better.

"Five-card stud," said Mark, leaning over the end of the table, his voice automatically establishing himself as a leader, one who would settle the inevitable disputes. "You get the first card face-down, then the next four cards up. Anyone got some questions, say now, 'cause we're playing for real." He paused for several seconds, almost dramatically. When nobody said anything, he continued, "How many chips you want, Charlie?"

Inexplicably, the young Baldwin's pulse began to race.

At fourteen, Charlie was two years older than the rest of the group. Although he was hefty and athletic, taking pride in winning, he was in no sense a bully. "Four bucks worth," he decided, and promptly received plastic chips of various colors—their values being announced by Mark.

Bobby bought in for six dollars and thirty-five cents. Steve reached into his pocket to purchase three-fifty worth of chips. Tom bought three dollars worth, and Mark paid for his chips with four rumpled dollar bills. So there it was—Bobby's first poker game—and he had the most money on the table.

But he didn't have the biggest bankroll. That honor went to Mark, their host. He was somewhat of a money hoarder, rumored to have almost $30 accumulated in a shoebox. But Mark was a cautious player and not apt to risk much of his fortune.

Bobby caught two 4s back-to-back on the first deal of Five-Stud. It seemed to him like a kiss from the gods of gambling. Surely it couldn't be a bad hand. Betting the 25-cent limit, he managed to eliminate everyone but Steve who had an ace showing. On the next card, Bobby caught a seven, Steve a queen. Neither player helped on the last two cards, but that queen had paired Steve's hole card. First hand. Lost. Worse than that, Bobby had impetuously called right down the line. Including the bet Bobby had lost when he'd led with his paired fours, the three bets he'd subsequently called, plus his nickel ante, the damage from hand one was $1.05.

He'd already lost 17% of his bankroll.

"Got anything to drink?" he asked his host, trying to act cool although he felt the first twist of a strange pain. It was a feeling he would learn to conquer . . . someday. It's a pain you keep to yourself. You get yourself into these messes, he reasoned. Only you can bail yourself out. No sense whining about it.

"Grape juice," Mark answered. "Just open the refrigerator and pour a glass."

He had no way of knowing that this would be a memorable day in his personal history. He did know that this was the first time he'd ever tasted grape juice. And he liked it.

♠

Sipping that grape juice gave me time to think. Gambling was a completely new experience. My heart was racing, but I tried to hide this fact from the others. I watched the next hand, standing close to Mark. But I wasn't really focusing. A peculiar excitement had gripped me. I liked poker already. Really liked it. And I'd have to leave this game soon to deliver newspapers. I didn't want to leave. Especially, I didn't want to leave losing! The $6.35 meant something to me. I had developed a pack-a-day cigarette habit, and even this meager sum of money (my first bankroll) had been squeezed out of my lunch money and my paper route profits. I'd saved it—and I sure didn't want to lose it in a matter of minutes. I psyched myself up, swallowed the last of my grape juice and returned to the game with determination.

♠

The next hand saw Bobby catch a second pair on the last card. That win made him almost even, and he considered quitting. But the small victory had bolstered his confidence.

Lying near his chips, where he could read it easily, he kept the insert card that came with the Hoyle deck. It told him the rankings of the hands, told him that a straight beats three-of-a-kind, told him that a full house beats a flush. The other players were slightly experienced and already knew this much. In fact, Mark had played numerous times and had even read a book on poker. The fact that he was out-experienced did not worry Baldwin. It just made him more determined. After a dozen hands, he had clearly established himself as the most aggressive player at the table. On the strength of two 3s he had got Charlie to lay down a pair of 7s. It was going to be easy, this poker, thought Bobby. You don't even need the best hand to win the money.

His whole being felt alive with this startling new discovery. He won three of the next five pots with the worst hand. Then the other players got wise. The strategy failed. His chips, which he had neatly stacked, began to disappear.

Then, as if the poker gods had granted him a reprieve, he got four cards to a flush against Mark's 7, 8, and 9 of hearts showing. Not only that, Bobby was trying for the *spade* flush—the best kind, judging by the elaborate design on the ace of spades. Charlie dealt each boy the final card. The 4 of hearts to Mark and the magic card, the ace of spades, to Bobby. It was a perfect catch for Baldwin. In his mind, there was no way Mark could have a better hand. In fact, the best hand his friend could possibly have was a heart flush. Bobby's spade flush would handle that.

Not so, he discovered a few seconds later, having gone all-in and exhausting his chips. Mark's flush was ace 9 high, Bobby's only ace 8. His friend was reaching for the pot.

"Wait!" cried the astounded Baldwin. "I've got a *spade* flush!"

"So what?" said Steve in a particularly whining voice that served to enrage Bobby all the more. "Mark's got a *higher* flush. Ain't supposed to be no argument about it. Deal the next hand."

It all seemed so brutal. His friend stacking the chips. No one wanting to hear Bobby's side of it. A feeling that, perhaps, he had been hustled. He tried to persist with his argument. But the next hand was being dealt—and Bobby, having no more ammunition to play with, was being dealt *out*!

♠

I delivered papers that day with a vengeance. I just couldn't get out of my mind the possibility that I'd been cheated. Somehow I'd got it stuck in my brain that spades was the super suit among cards. And if I could find evidence to this effect, I was going to march right back over to Mark's house and demand a prompt return of my money. It was this that I had in mind as I flung paper after paper at their designated porches. In my exasperated anger, I managed to land three of the papers on rooftops—something I had rarely ever done.

Having completed my route, I hurried toward the library. I would need to hurry. Find a poker book and hurry back to Mark's with my documentation before the game adjourned —if it hadn't already. Hoyle's seemed like the ideal reference book, since it had been a Hoyle deck they'd *used to rape me of my $6.35. I remembered the insert card I'd kept beside me while playing, the card that defined the ranks of poker hands. Had it said anything about the value of the various suits? In the heat of the argument (which Charlie, the oldest and strongest, had eventually settled just by standing up and glaring menacingly), I hadn't thought to look at that card. But a tremor of worry registered with me. I sure hadn't noticed any mention of spades beating hearts. I had good reason to worry, I discovered. Within five minutes I'd located the book I wanted. But Hoyle made no mention of the suits having different value.*

My pockets were empty. My ego was hurting. How could I redeem my self-image?

I've always been a highly competitive person. It's just my nature. And there's some weakness because of it. Whenever I've gone broke, I've just geared down and started from scratch. Even at twelve years old, this philosophy felt right to me. I had lost over six dollars, and it hurt. But it made me stubborn. Somehow I was going to beat poker. Especially, I was going to devote myself to beating Mark, my friend who had taken my money.

Reflecting on that first game, I saw how it emphasized several mistakes that beginning players habitually make.

1. The majority of neophyte poker players attribute their loss to a bad run of cards. That's what I did. Poker is the great game it is because, although it deceives weak players into believing it is a game of luck, it is primarily a game of skill. When you're able to rationalize that the money you lost was a stroke of bad fortune, you're willing to stubbornly charge back into the next game feeling that fate, which was so cruel to you at the previous session, now owes you a favor. So it was with me.

2. Being hard-headed, I played too loose. And there's a world of difference between playing an aggressive, scientific game and just plain playing loose. It's the difference between a dynamic poker professional and a perpetual caller who goes home busted night after night. I began as a habitual caller. Hard headed. Couldn't lay down a hand in that first session at Mark's house. Wanted to bull the game, but didn't know how. Called right down to the last cards without any knowledge of probability.

If I got tied to a hand, I'd end up going all-in with it. I'd play my chips right down to the table top, because there was no such thing as backing down. No value laydowns. No discretion.

3. You can't play for so much money that it bothers your concentration. You end up spending your mental energy on thinking about money and not about strategy. There is the other extreme, too: Play for matchsticks or play for too little money and you don't make critical decisions because it doesn't mean anything.

4. I treated gambling as a diversion—an escape from ordinary reality. When you take poker seriously, you've got to honor the game. It's an art form. When you need to escape, choose other forms of recreation.

5. Bad players tend to get themselves into situations where they lose more than they should when they get a hand beat and don't win enough when they take a pot. So it was with me at Mark's house. I called right down to the last card too many times when it was almost hopeless. Because I wasn't sure when I had the nuts, I missed several betting opportunities.

6. The more comfortable you are, the better you'll perform. Wear loose fitting clothes. That was one thing I accidentally did right. But I made myself uncomfortable just by playing when I knew I had to leave to deliver papers. Deadlines tend to be so psychologically devastating to unskilled players who are losing that many pros have devised strategies to take advantage of this fact. As the losing player is threatened with the termination of the game, he tries desperately to get even. He plays recklessly. Usually he loses a lot more than he should in his futile attempt to recover in a short time. You'll see this happen when you're playing in a public casino that's about to close, or in a home game with a predetermined cutoff. I've known great players who lied, telling a weak losing opponent that they had to leave in twenty minutes. When the twenty minutes expired, they just found some phony reason why they didn't have to quit the game after all.

Anyway, I spent the next few days steaming over my first poker loss. For some reason, the pain was so great that I had trouble sleeping. I managed to squeeze together a few bucks for a second poker game with the same group. Lost again, every penny. So I plotted, but there was no *other poker game for weeks. I did learn a new kind of gambling: Dice at Charlie's house. This time it was purely a game of luck. Just the two of us played. We started out at 25¢ roll, ended up at $1 a roll. I got lucky. Pocketing my $8 winnings, I was ready for Mark—ready to play poker. Still, I didn't have any technical knowledge of the game. I was oblivious to the fact that there was technical knowledge to be known. So, confidently, I cornered Mark in the school cafeteria and challenged him. Heads-up, five-card stud. His house.*

♠

There was no serious grudge between them. The hostility Bobby had first felt was fading. But in its place was a keen competitive yearning. For Baldwin, this second poker confrontation held all the drama of an important athletic event. He had never psyched himself higher. There would be no audience, but he could hear a ghostly crowd screaming for his victory. Cheers heaped upon cheers, all spirit-like and known only to himself. So he marched into Mark's house with a single purpose. His gait was brisker than usual. He was going to be a hero in his own eyes. This he knew. This was certain. It was as if the demolition of Mark in the kitchen battlefield of poker was a thing already done. He had convinced himself he would win. All that remained was to do it.

It was the same Hoyle deck they'd used last time. They even sat in the same chairs, although without Charlie and the others there, they might have seated themselves anywhere.

FREEZE OUT

Just as before, they agreed to nickel ante with a quarter limit. Each boy started with $5 worth of chips. This time they added the stipulation that it would be freeze-out. That meant the game couldn't end until someone won all the chips on the table.

"That might take hours, though," Mark pointed out. It was Saturday morning at eleven o'clock, and they had a whole day to waste.

"Might," Bobby agreed. But secretly he thought Mark's comment absurd. Baldwin was determined to win the chips in as short a time as possible.

"Cut. High card deals," said Mark. And he promptly beat Bobby's 7 with a 10.

That was just about the last good thing that happened to the somewhat cocky Mark. First hand. Bobby caught a third 6 and shot down a pair of aces. Next hand. Bobby started with paired kings, and they held up. Third hand. Mark tried for a flush and paired aces. Not good enough to beat Bobby's 8s and 6s. And then the fourth and final hand. Mark had two jacks after three cards, finishing with jacks-up and losing to Baldwin's flush.

MORE MONEY

"You keep drawing out on me," Mark complained, using the poker term often reserved for complaints. It means that an opponent had the worst hand during the initial betting stages, but got lucky enough to improve along the way and win the pot. He *drew out*.

Bobby could see how upset his friend had become over a $5 loss. He always figured Mark to end up as a miser, running some small business somewhere and keeping books on every penny.

"Wanna watch some football?" Bobby suggested, getting up from the table and stuffing the two five-dollar bills—which had been placed at the far edge of the table for the winner—into his pocket.

"You quitting?" asked Mark nervously. It was clear that he had caught the same fever that usually strikes gamblers once they get behind. They become hooked and their rational mind breaks apart, almost visibly. Here as steady, money-hoarding Mark sounding desperate with the fear that this game might not continue. He might not have a chance to get even.

"Got any more money?" Baldwin asked casually. He knew Mark had more money. He kept it beneath his bed in a shoebox. And suddenly Baldwin was eager for the kill. He wanted that money.

"Be right back." Mark exited the kitchen, trying to act cool, trying to walk in a normal manner. But the boy was clearly unnerved, almost striding on his toes in an effort to reach the bedroom and his shoebox before Baldwin changed his mind.

They played another $5 freeze-out. This one took Bobby twenty minutes to win. Mark was shaking now, and he went to get more money.

Ten minutes and that was lost.

Mark sat stunned for a long time, struggling not to show the hurt. But his eyes were directed at the table in front of him, vacant of chips. It was as if he were fighting off tears, but Bobby couldn't be sure.

When, finally, someone spoke, it was Mark saying, "My folks oughta be home soon, so I only got time for once more." His voice cracked, but he swallowed and then coughed in an effort to cover up. "So maybe ... if you want to ... we could play for ... fifteen, and then it would be double or nothing."

Baldwin had to think this over. He knew he had Mark in a bad way psychologically. Everything had gone smoothly so far. But he wished Mark had suggested they play for $10. That way Bobby could lose this final freeze out and still score a profit. But the challenge had been made. Now it was his choice to either accept or reject it.

"If you're sure you want to risk it," Bobby said.

THE END OF MARK

It was a brutal finish. Within fifteen minutes, Mark was all-in. Bobby had aces from the beginning. Mark was trailing with two 8s after the third card. Last card. Baldwin turned each over slowly, dramatically. It was as if he were parroting some scene from an old western movie. But the drama died suddenly when Mark's card failed to help. Bobby made aces-up, but that was irrelevant.

"Play some more," Mark urged. "I ain't got it right now, but I'll owe it to you."

They played for $10. It was solemnly agreed that it would be the last game, no matter what. After that was lost, Mark cast an imploring look toward Baldwin. He couldn't ask to play again. That would be less than honorable. But it's hard to maintain honor under stress. Especially for a twelve-year-old miser who is suddenly penniless. Still, Mark refrained from begging. Instead he tried to convey pity. But Baldwin declined to respond to this emotional blackmail. He did pat Mark affectionately on the back.

"Could you . . . could you loan me $5? My mom's gonna have a birthday and . . ." The last of Mark's words were obscured by a semi-deliberate mumble.

Bobby gave his friend the money and left. He had twenty-five dollars more now than when he'd ridden his bike over to Mark's. Plus, he was owed fifteen more. He'd even learned how to check a winning hand and let an opponent do his betting for him. It was called checking-and-raising or, more commonly, sandbagging. He'd done it, and it had paid off. Poker was going to be easy.

My exaltation was not merited by my play. I'd drawn out on Mark more often than he'd drawn out on me, gone in with the worst hand repeatedly and come out best. Of course, I didn't realize this at the time. I was floating on a cloud, but I was destined to fall through it.

Some things I had done right. For the first time in my life, I'd sandbagged a hand that Saturday afternoon. It had worked perfectly. Also, I'd agreed to play for that double-or-nothing freeze-out. And even though Mark was the better player, mine was the right decision. He was psychologically beaten. I think he knew he was going to lose. He played several hands terribly, even though he knew better. He was desperate, and I'd taken advantage of that.

But I wasn't ready to win at poker. I didn't even understand the fundamentals of a game as uncomplicated as Five-Stud. That game is seldom played seriously in big-time poker today. But, because it's a game made popular by movies and dealt in friendly home games, I'm going to discuss it briefly. Since it was the first form of poker I ever played, this would be an appropriate time to talk about it. I'll tell you what the most common mistakes are and then provide you with a very simple winning formula.

Before I do this, I want to point out that in the popular movie, The Cincinnati Kid, the Kid makes a gigantic mistake which costs him the world title: That's in spite of the fact that it was the most realistic, well researched and expensive poker movie of all time! I'll tell you about that mistake shortly.

CHAPTER 3

Five-Card Stud

Yes, Five-Stud is the simplest popular form of poker. Even so, in the movie The Cincinnati Kid, *Steve McQueen (the Kid) was challenging Edward G. Robinson (the Man) for the championship of the world.*

After four cards the Kid had aces-up and the very best the Man could have was a pair of queens. Also, the Man could have been playing for a straight-flush. Instead of tapping the Man off in this situation, or at least betting enough so that it would not be profitable for him to call, the Kid let the reigning champ off for a few thousand dollars, not a large amount when weighed against the size of the pot.

Kid's motive? Apparently, he figured the Man for a pair of queens and wanted to convey the image of having only the vulnerable pair of 10s, which were exposed on his board. This is an almost ludicrous bit of judgment, because if the Man did have the pair of queens, he could probably have been forced to call a large raise then. If the Man were trying for a flush, even a straight-flush, the Kid ought to have taxed him dearly for the privilege of seeing a fifth card. The Kid probably should have bet every dollar and whatever line of credit was available to him. It's likely that his decision to play soft on fourth street cost the Kid the world title.

COMMON MISTAKES

MISTAKE ONE:
Playing small hole cards

When you have an ace up and a 6 in the hole, you're pretty much out to lunch against a bettor starting the hand with a 7 showing. Unsophisticated players make this mistake all the time. What possible hand could the bettor be playing that is inferior to yours? King 7? Hardly! He's looking at an ace. Unless you think he's bluffing, throw your hand away.

MISTAKE TWO:
Slow playing small pairs

When you're fortunate enough to start off with a pair of 5s, don't wait cleverly in the bushes until someone draws out on you. That's called "slow playing," and this is a time when it's wrong. Try to limit the field of opposition. Try to get in a head-up situation, if possible. A pair of 5s is a substantial favorite against ace-king.

MISTAKE THREE:
Overplaying an ace in the hole

This might be the most frequent mistake among Five-Stud players. It's nice to have a concealed ace, but many players just fall in love with it and let go of a hand when they're clearly beaten.

MISTAKE FOUR:
Trying for straights and flushes

Particularly seven stud players have this fault. In Five-Stud, you don't have twenty-one different combinations of cards from which to select your best hand—as is the case in Seven-Stud. You have just one combination: the five cards you end up with. You should never be influenced to start with a hand because your first two cards are suited. The odds against making the flush are almost 120 to 1. Clearly the most important consideration should be the size of your cards relative to the other cards exposed. Even if your first three cards are suited, it is seldom profitable to call a bet unless your cards are big enough to merit that action. Straights are even worse to try for than flushes.

FINAL FORMULA

RULE ONE:

Anytime you begin without a pair, your hole card must be as big as anything showing.

RULE TWO:

If you start with a small pair, play it very aggressively on the first round of betting.

RULE THREE:

Never call a normal-to-large bet with three small suited cards, unless there's a straight-flush possibility.

RULE FOUR:

If you haven't paired after three cards and appear to have the weaker board, fold.

RULE FIVE:

Don't play for straights or flushes.

CHAPTER 4

A New Hobby

Over the next two years, Bobby played poker only half a dozen times. Nothing more than quarter limit. He never lost more than three dollars and never won more than five. It wasn't that he didn't like poker. He was crazy about it. Unfortunately, his affinity for the game was not equaled by his friends.

He did develop a new hobby that satisfied his competitive needs. It was pool. There were those rare poker games, occasionally dice, and even a dollar wagered now and then on football. But mostly it was pool.

Almost from the first time he held a cue stick, Baldwin was confident and accurate. The balls just started falling in the pockets. At first he'd line up every shot, the way he'd been instructed. You take the cue stick in your right hand and point it toward the pocket. Visualize the point where the line from the pocket crosses the nearest side of the target ball. Draw another line from that spot to the cue ball, and you shoot straight along that second line.

Well, Bobby used this method for about fifteen minutes. It worked okay, but he had a method that worked better. Instinct. He just knew where to hit the balls so that they'd cleanly spill into the pockets. And the sight of those colorful spheres disappearing from the table excited him. He was addicted after his first practice session.

But on his second excursion to Doc's Pool Hall, a dusty basement establishment, he got arrested.

A MAJOR BUST

Bobby and an older boy were gambling on nine-ball. Bobby had won six games in a row at fifty cents each, leaping from a dollar-fifty loser to a dollar-fifty winner. The lanky lad he was challenging kept slamming his cue stick against a nearby table and swearing.

The rule was you had to call your shot on the nine ball. So Bobby, standing at one end of the table, took sight on the three ball down at the other end and declared that, after a complex chain of events, the seven-ball would knock the nine ball into the nearest side pocket.

The lanky kid scoffed. "Yeah, well if you make that mother, I quit!"

Bobby shot. The front basement door swung open and four policemen charged briskly into Doc's. The nine ball sank cleanly into the pocket. Bobby clenched his fist victoriously. The other kid threw his cue stick against the floor. It bounced up and crashed against his knee.

"Ow! Damn it!" he cried. Then he reached into his pocket for two quarters which he hurled onto the pool table. Bobby put these into his pocket just in time. The party was over.

Like criminals, Bobby and four other young-looking boys were lined up against a wall. Frisked, pockets emptied.

"Stand still, boy!" barked the biggest, gruffest cop. And, although, by nature, Bobby is not easily intimidated, he stood very, very still.

An hour later he and two of the other boys from the pool hall were at the local police station waiting for their parents to arrive. You see, it was against the law in Tulsa for anyone under the mature age of sixteen to be caught in a pool hall. And Bobby Baldwin, although he would later become poker champ of the world and a good citizen, had been caught and arrested. His name tarnished at fourteen.

♠

We were treated like real criminals when we got to the police station. Like robbers. Like hoodlums: My parents were liberal and caring. Almost ideal parents, thinking back on it. But the mother of one of the other kids who got arrested went completely crazy. I mean, her kid was only thirteen years old and she acted like he'd been accused of a hideous mass murder.

"How could you do this, Timmy?" she shrieked. "Your father will die when he finds out. Just die, I tell you. We were going to get you a bike for your birthday, too. Well, if you think your father is going to slave at the office all day to get you a bike after this, you better think again, mister!"

Real tears were flooding his eyes. I waited for her wrath to boil itself out and for her motherly tenderness to surface.

"You ain't even a boy, you're an animal!" she screamed even louder than before. By now everyone was looking, and Timmy's tears popped into his eyes even bigger than before.

The woman was silent for several seconds, but then the bombardment resumed. "Handcuffs!" she howled. Then there was another short silence as the import of her last word seemed to strike her. "Oh my God! They brought you here in handcuffs. Do you know who gets to wear handcuffs? Huh? Huh? Don't answer, you sniveling little brat! I'll tell you who. Nazis, that's who, and safecrackers and pornographers. Just wait till your father hears this!" Finally, lacking the stamina to continue her assault, she collapsed sobbing on a wooden bench. Timmy, too, was crying fitfully. A sergeant came over and placed a hand softly on her shoulder to offer comfort. She grabbed at the hand and hurled it away.

"Look what you've done to my son!"

Luckily none of us gained any permanent criminal record. They had secured us with handcuffs just like big time crooks, fingerprinted us and locked us in a cell. But they had every right to do it. We were underage.

Escorted home by my parents (who for some reason didn't take the episode too seriously), I resolved not to go to Doc's Pool Hall again till I turned sixteen.

I'd learned my lesson.

One thing I think this pool hall account emphasizes is that you have to be careful where you go to gamble. Poker today is not considered a criminal activity in the public's opinion. And enlightened police forces across the country are generally very reluctant to raid a "friendly" poker game. But that doesn't mean you should just sit down anywhere and feel secure. Cities, states, and counties have vastly different laws. And the vigor with which police enforce them varies as widely as the laws themselves.

The same is true of the trouble I got myself into at Doc's. Sure, being underage at a pool hall is not much of an offense in most folks' minds. But the police in Tulsa thought it was a big deal, and that was public knowledge. I should have exercised more discretion.

Police aren't the only (or even the major) fear you have when you attend private poker games. The country is filled with hijackers—thieves who prey on the games, barging in with everything from shotguns and knives to machine guns.

Anyway, like I said, I'd learned my lesson.

In fact, Bobby didn't play pool again for two full days. Well, that wasn't exactly eons, but it did show that he was somewhat frightened by the rough handling he'd suffered at the hands of the Tulsa police. It was his brother Kenny who talked him into frequenting a more modern pool hall. Seems the police tended to concentrate their raids on the seedier establishments, the old-style, dingy, male-only halls that often had illegal gin games in back rooms. In the case of Doc's, it was dominoes.

Kenny's theory was that there would be a margin of safety in playing at the new Cue Center. It was located in a busy shopping center with a "wholesome" atmosphere and even catered to women. That latter fact mattered more to Kenny who was nineteen than to the younger Baldwin whose interest in girls was then only moderate.

So it was at the Cue Center that Bobby practiced and polished his game until he'd become one of the best shooters in the neighborhood. Still more practice. Within a year, Bobby could handle *anybody* who set foot in the Center. Now and then he'd sneak into Doc's, never again to be arrested there.

Then came an experience that would profoundly mold the way he'd represent himself as a gambler. Until it happened, he'd always felt that if circumstances were just right and he had a chance at a big pool score, he'd hustle his way into it. Missing easy shots, waiting till the stakes got high. Then striking the cue ball with sudden accuracy. After all, that was the way everyone else did it, wasn't it?

AN ENLIGHTENMENT

The kid's name was Danny, and he was the same age as Bobby. One Saturday afternoon, Bobby came home to find his twin brother and Danny playing chess on the living room carpet. Now, Billy looks a lot like Bobby, though they aren't identical twins. Back then, they were dissimilar in that Billy was more into intellectual endeavors—chess, for instance—while Bobby cared about pool halls and hanging out with the boys.

Danny was in the process of losing his fourth consecutive game, but he took the defeats good-naturedly. "You're just too good for me, Billy," he acknowledged.

"Let's do something else," Billy suggested. "Hi, Bobby. We were playing a little chess."

Seemed obvious, so Bobby didn't comment.

"*What* else?" Danny wanted to know.

Each suggested several activities: electric football, walking down to the shopping center, checkers, Monopoly. Nothing was decided.

Then Danny said, "Ever shot any pool."

"Not much," Billy said.

"I been playing quite a bit lately," Danny said.

Bobby interrupted, "That's what I heard. Heard you lost six bucks to Big Kevin yesterday."

"Yeah," Danny admitted matter-of-factly, "Kev's pretty good. Why don't you an' me play some."

Had Bobby Baldwin been a hustler at heart, he would have jumped to the challenge, perhaps even conned the inexperienced Danny into spotting a ball or two. Instead, a part of his true nature leapt to the forefront.

He said, "It wouldn't be fair. You can't beat Big Kevin, and I'm a lot better than he is. You'd just lose your money."

Danny sat for twenty seconds thinking it over. "You're probably right," he said at last. "But I think I'll give it a try." Five minutes later, dragging Billy along as a "scorekeeper" so as not to make him feel abandoned, they set out for the Cue Center.

THE CUE CENTER

I won the first seven games at a quarter each. You'd think Danny would consider quitting or at least ask for some sort of spot. No. He actually seemed to enjoy the tension. Finally, I got to feeling ridiculous. It was just too easy.

I said, "Why don't you quit. Or we can just play for the fun of it."

"Let's play for a half buck a game," he suggested in a tone of voice that indicated he was offering some sort of a compromise.

Danny had quite a bit of money in his pocket. I'd guess twelve to fifteen dollars. And although I wanted to win it, I felt that the game we'd agreed to was totally unfair.

"Tell you what. I'll spot you the eight and seven balls and we'll play ten games. Fifty cents a game. Okay?"

I think this concept of fairness has always been a basic part of my gambling nature. Many big-time gamblers, and even some of my friends who are gamblers, tend to seek the very best they can get out of every wagering situation. If that means lying back and pretending they're less accomplished at a game than they really are, that's the strategy they employ. I have nothing against that approach. In fact, I get a vicarious thrill out of the legendary exploits of Titanic Thompson and other great hustlers.

Hustling just isn't my way of doing things. For me, it doesn't feel right. The personal gambling creed I live by today is: Never misrepresent yourself. Take pride in the poker skills you've acquired, and always play your toughest game.

Nothing cemented that notion in my mind as much as that Saturday afternoon at the Cue Center. Danny just wouldn't quit.

They'd agreed to play only ten games, but Bobby had already claimed the first five and you could tell Danny would not want to hang his cue stick back on the rack after the next five.

A small crowd was lingering around the table.

"If you guys are gonna quit pretty soon," said a husky kid wearing a high school letterman's jacket, "I'll play some with you, Danny."

Danny, distracted by the older boy's remark, connected sloppily with the cue ball which barely struck the nearby seven ball at which he'd been aiming. Nevertheless, the off-target seven ball brushed the eight ball, which nudged the nine ball, which whispered into the side pocket.

"I win!" Danny was exhilarated by this first success in over a half hour of competition against Baldwin.

"Real nice shot," the older youth chided while several of the other onlookers afforded Danny a sarcastic sprinkling of applause. "You gonna play me or not?"

"Naw."

"Why not? I ain't no good. Ask anyone."

Danny looked away from lining up his break shot to find three pals of the older kid all nodding vigorously. "Yes," they were saying wordlessly, "he isn't any good, you can beat him." No doubt, Danny didn't even recognize this as a hustle by conspiracy. But in his mind, it didn't matter whether a new opponent would be easier competition. It was Bobby he wanted to play. And even though impossible, it was Bobby he wanted to beat.

Danny lost all his money, played on credit and ended up owing Bobby $11 by five o'clock when they quit. It was only the first of dozens of pool battles between the two. Baldwin tried to be fair in setting up the spots. But it was useless. Danny just never won.

CHAPTER 5

Hustlers

I began to feel sorry for Danny. The other regulars who hung out at the Cue Center kept chiding him. They had a pet name for him: Bobby's Goose.

"Here comes Bobby's Goose!" they'd say when he walked through the door. And when I was there without him, they'd say, "Where's your goose today?"

I got to feeling a closeness for Danny, and we became friends. I finally had to refuse to play Danny for big money. But there were a lot of others to play, and I had developed a reputation as the best shooter at the Cue Center. My reputation hadn't prevented Danny from playing me, and it was no deterrent to anyone else. All through high school, I kept money in my pockets by playing pool. But not from hustling pool. I never hustled. Never, and I'm proud of it.

I can say the same about poker. Some people have temperaments that make it impossible for someone to enjoy playing against them. At poker, they throw cards and insult weaker opponents. "How could you possibly make that call?" they'll say, instead of losing graciously. "Don't you even know enough not to play that hand against a double raise?" At pool, they slam their cue sticks into the table and swear at lesser players. "That's the luckiest shooting I've ever seen. You couldn't beat my grandma if you didn't keep slopping in the nine ball. With your luck, I shouldn't be spotting you anything!"

People with that kind of disposition are invariably hustlers. Hustling is the only way they can get action. But why should anyone play against a much stronger opponent if the experience figures to be unpleasant?

49

If there's one plain truth I've discovered about gambling, it's this: GAMBLERS ENJOY A CHALLENGE. They'll play you because you are good. They'll seek you out, suggest a game and lose politely. Perhaps, in their minds, they leave richer because of the experience. In order to get weaker opponents to want to play against you, though, you've got to be honorable. That means you must have a reputation for always paying your debts, for never cheating and never hustling. Beyond that, you must be pleasant to play against, win or lose. With that magic combination, you'll find very few poker games (or any sort of gambling propositions) that you'll be excluded from simply because you're an accomplished player.

It's important that you remember:

1. Be friendly. Don't lose your temper.

2: Never hustle.

I've been invited to countless games just because of my reputation as a top-rated poker professional. And ever since I won the world championship, I've been flooded with offers to play in private games across the nation. I get dozens of heads-up offers every week. These people don't feel they have the best of it. They know they're outclassed.

But, for the most part, they've developed a degree of poker skill and want the excitement of testing it against the finest competition they can find.

One last and important thought here. There are no "suckers" in poker. I can't count the number of times that lower-level poker pros use that term to describe some guy who's sitting across the table throwing off a few grand on seemingly outrageous plays.

More often than not, the "sucker" is a $75,000-a-year executive and the "pro" is struggling to earn his $30,000 annually at the poker tables. Remember, these players are taking the game recreationally. You're taking it seriously. You shouldn't ridicule them for not knowing the in's and out's of your profession any more than they should criticize you for not understanding theirs.

RETURN TO DOC'S

This was one of Bobby's now rare visits to Doc's Pool Hall. Even though the Cue Center was modern, with better tables and a happier atmosphere, there was something comforting about the dusty basement pool hall—something that occasionally lured Baldwin back. Even the fear of being arrested again was not enough to keep him away. Besides, another seven months and he wouldn't be underage any more. At sixteen, he could visit Doc's legally. In the meantime, today, he was clicking ball after ball into the intended pockets, practicing one of the two games he loved. Poker was the other, but there hadn't been many opportunities lately to try his luck at that.

Cigar smoke breezed across the low ceilings, weaving diaphanous designs beneath the hanging lights. It was downright dingy. Mysterious, like a movie scene where some gangster waits to make his dramatic entrance.

Enter a man in a business suit.

He scanned the room briefly, noting that there were just three tables in use. Within minutes he was using the table alongside the one where Bobby was practicing. The well-dressed newcomer wasn't bad. Not bad at all, but Bobby was better.

"Bet you don't get many strangers in here." the man said.

"Not too many," said Baldwin.

"Like to shoot some? I'm just passing through town."

"What game you like to play?" Bobby was giving the guy a careful appraisal: Expensive clothes, about forty, wearing glasses. He seemed to be a respectable-looking businessman.

"Nine ball's okay. Dollar a ball?"

"Let's start out at a half," said Bobby. Although he never hustled, he was always on guard against being hustled.

The stranger took a wooden cue stick off the rack, rolled it across the table and decided it was too warped for his liking. He tested several more before he found one he considered acceptable, though, even then he grumbled about its quality.

After ten games, Bobby and the businessman were even. Then the man missed several easy shots during the next five games. Bobby was a buck and a half ahead.

It was getting late when the well-dressed man said, "You know I got a stick in the car I never used before. Client sold it to me for five bucks." He took a business card from an inside pocket of his suit jacket and handed it to Baldwin. An insurance salesman. "I think I'll run outside and get it. These sticks around here are hardly worth beans."

Bobby was fairly certain then that the man was hustling, although he lost the first game using his fancy stick. Now Bobby was two dollars ahead, and the insurance man wanted to play for a dollar a game.

Bobby figured he'd play it and then quit if the man won the money back. Sure enough, the stranger suddenly turned into a super shooter, banking in balls at amazing angles and sinking three-ball combinations. But it wasn't enough.

They ended up playing for five dollars a ball, with Bobby winning almost every game. The easy-going, soft-spoken salesman, who had entered the pool room three hours ago, was getting angrier and grumpier.

"Jesus, kid! Don't you ever miss?" he bellowed. Twice he smashed his cue stick against the wall and once he was so enraged that he needed to take a ten minute walk. For "fresh air" he said, but when he returned, there was the unmistakable scent of liquor on his breath.

His anger seemed to lighten then, and the man took his defeat almost philosophically. Finally, owing $130, he'd had enough.

"I don't have my checkbook with me," he said. "Follow me down to the grocery store up the road. They have customer checks there. I'll write you one. Young man, you sure are some pool shooter!"

Bobby had never accepted a personal check before, except from his paper route customers—and those were not written to him, but to the newspaper. But here was a respectable adult businessman, and if ever Bobby was to take the plunge into the big world of grown-up finance, this seemed like the time.

Since Bobby didn't have a car, the man drove him to the grocery store, wrote the check out neatly, including his account number and the words "pool game" in the bottom left-hand corner.

This was a *friendly* transaction. They shook hands. Bobby felt euphoric: This was the most money he'd ever won gambling. In his pocket he had the $46 (most of what he'd started the day with) and a check for $130: The next day he spent $30 on a portable radio. After all, he could easily afford it.

He had his parents deposit the check at their bank. It bounced a week later. There was no such account.

♠

Some of the most perplexing decisions a gambler has to make involve lending, borrowing and cashing checks. There seems to be no hard, fast rules that will cover any situation. But here are some thoughts:

Looking at the pool hall situation with the insurance agent, my naivety caused me to handle it poorly.

First, you don't ever trust someone who hasn't previously established himself as honorable. Making an assumption that a person is honest because he appears to be dressed respectably can be a serious mistake. However, even professional gamblers allow themselves to be victims of extending credit too liberally. It's awfully hard to say "no" when the person asking for the loan, or asking you to cash a check, is a nice person.

Rule One: Never lend money on the basis of whether it's to a "nice guy."

Second, you should keep your mind specifically tuned to detect arising credit impasses. After the insurance salesman got five or so dollars behind and mentioned nothing about how he intended to pay, it should have been obvious to me that I was headed straight for a payment problem. I was deluded into feeling that, because the man appeared well-to-do, he was honorable.

Rule Two: Don't feel embarrassed about asking questions regarding when and how you're going to get paid.

Only a person with dishonorable intentions will be annoyed by such questions. When you have to ask, there is a good chance that your opponent's credit standing might be shaky. Most gamblers with good intentions will never leave you wondering how or whether you're going to get paid.

Third, you should ask for collateral. The salesman was wearing an expensive watch. Instead of cashing his check, I could have politely agreed to hold the watch for him until he returned with the money. Most losers are more than willing to do this, since it relieves them of the social pressure of owing money.

Rule Three: Only accept paper or promises from strangers where no other means of payment is available.

Fourth, you must control people who can't control themselves. This means you should seldom get yourself in a situation where you have to worry about getting paid. Because of the fear of hijackings, most major private poker games are played on paper. That is, no cash changes hands at the sight of the game. Usually, the man who runs the game keeps careful track of all transactions. But I've seen time after time where a man who was willing to lose two thousand a week, and could afford it, lost twenty thousand because he was given more credit than he could handle comfortably.

When you give a man more credit than he feels at ease with, that's just madness. When you give him $20,000 credit instead of $3,000 and he loses the big number, very frequently he won't be able to pay. Then what? Usually, you don't even get the $3,000 you would have collected had you cut off the credit line early. Worse still, the guy is not likely to ever show up at that game again. Next week he'll lose his two grand elsewhere.

When you think a guy has lost enough, just say, "Sorry, Henry, that's as much as I can do for you tonight. You really had a bad run of cards. I hope you do better next week." Henry will almost always accept that as final. If he doesn't, you've got to stand firm.

When the insurance salesman started losing over twenty dollars, I should have insisted on payment then. Even if he'd had to write me a check, it might well have been a good one on an existing account. I would have been twenty dollars richer, he would still have felt honorable, and he may have returned to Doc's to lose again.

Rule Four: Try never to be the cause of a player overextending his credit.

Once you establish a worthy reputation in the poker world, you'll have limitless invitations to private games. Your word will be respected, and like all leading professionals, you will seldom need to take cash to these games. You'll want to establish your credit in advance, though. Tell the houseman that you intend to sit in on his next game. Specify how much credit you want, and never go beyond that limit. Remember, credit at games is a courtesy extended solely on the basis of your reputation. You must remain honorable. Always.

Once you've established a worthy reputation, you'll be able to borrow without having to repay immediately. Occasionally, I've been short of accessible funds. I'll approach the houseman and say, "I'd like to play in your game next week, and I'd need $20,000 credit. But I won't be able to pay it back for thirty days."

The houseman will say, "That's fine, Bobby. See you next week." Honor is everything to a gambler. You always say in advance that you're going to be late in paying. You never give a reason. None is expected of you.

Another related concept is: You should be suspicious of anyone giving elaborate excuses about why they can't pay. If you can't trust them just on their word without any explanation, don't trust them at all.

Among professional poker players, you frequently extend credit, but you never accept a percentage. Juice isn't expected or paid. That's just the way it is in the world of poker professionals. You ask favors selectively; you do favors selectively.

Important: The safest games you can play in are ones that are run entirely on credit. Your chances of being hijacked are almost nonexistent. Since these are games of honor, and since honor is the backbone of the winning pro gambler, you can figure to almost always get paid. Almost?

Yes, once I got stiffed for $15,000. That's the cost of being in the traveling poker business.

Before you even consider lending money, you must know the reputation of the person. In other words, that reputation must be positive. Just the fact that you know nothing negative is not reason enough to take a chance on a stranger.

Most people make the mistake of lending money when they feel that they will probably get repaid. Well, probably won't do it, brother! You have to feel absolutely certain. If you feel it's 3 to 1 likely that a person will repay the money he wants to borrow . . . well, that's a terrible proposition. If you did that with a hundred people at $10,000 a try, you'd only expect to get $750,000 back out of a million dollars in loans. Sure, 75% of the people proved honorable. Some consolation!

One of the biggest mistakes you can make is to feel obligated to lend on the basis of whether you think someone is probably honorable. Be sure or don't lend money. Naturally, this makes your life a little complicated. It's hard to turn somebody down who has been friendly toward you. In fact, it hurts. But you've got to do it. And don't give an elaborate explanation, either. Just say, "Sorry," and smile politely.

Only borrow from those you're willing to lend to, and don't lend to those who won't help others when they have the chance. It goes both ways. Many people want to borrow when you're up, but don't want to lend when you're down.

Another thing to consider is, there are a lot of people who habitually borrow, say, $500. They're always good for it, but they always borrow it back again. This may seem like an acceptable situation. But, in truth, the use of that money is lost to you forever.

The bottom line is this: Lending, borrowing, accepting checks and taking markers are all personal decisions. Be generous, but don't let social pressure dictate your decisions.

When you think of gambling as your business, you also think of money as the machinery that keeps that business operating. It would be nice if you could let everyone use it, but basically you've got to use it yourself.

CHAPTER 6

A Gold Rush

By late in his sophomore year, Bobby's skill at pool had reached the stage where he could conquer anyone in his high school. In fact, he could beat just about anybody who limped into Doc's or the Cue Center. His near mastery of the game insured him that he always had pocket money. Instead of taking the worst of it, as he had in his first poker sessions, he was always getting the best of it. At pool, the odds were working in his favor. On the negative side, his interest in school was fading.

He'd begun hanging around with a wild, but not totally malicious, crowd. They'd borrow statues from front yards, trade them with other statues belonging to neighboring houses and camp out in cars to watch the owners' reaction the next morning. Playful, kid stuff. Bobby was missing a lot of school. More often than not, when he skipped classes he'd end up at the pool hall. His report card showed the decline in his attendance. His parents, though worried, remained understanding.

He had a steady girlfriend named Carolyn. She was fun and attractive, with access to her parents' car. Because she was six months older than Bobby, she already had her driver's license, while Bobby only had a learner's permit. Her parents liked Bobby and quietly accepted the fact that *he* was driving when he dated their daughter.

"We're going to be late," Carolyn worried one morning as Bobby drove her into the school parking lot.

"Not if we hurry. Get your books ready. We'll just squeeze your folk's trusty vehicle into that spot there and make a mad dash for the classroom."

"You can't fit this car in that space!"

Girls are silly, thought Baldwin, courageously yanking the steering wheel and aiming the car perfectly into the parking space.

"Bobby, stop!"

"Why?" Crash! "Damn! Just run along to class, Carolyn. No sense both of us being late."

Luck had it that there was no damage to Carolyn's parents' car, but there was a large dent in the side of the car adjoining. He'd barely kissed it, like brushing a nine ball into a side pocket. Still, there it was, a noticeable dent.

Being honorable, Bobby jotted down the license number, checked with the dean's office and found out who the car belonged to. It was a senior.

In a quiet hallway outside the chemistry lab, Bobby confessed his misdeed to the older boy. The kid was understanding. Bobby told him to get an estimate, promising to promptly pay the damages.

It came to $100. Baldwin only had $15 or so at the time, and he didn't want to tell his parents, especially since he wasn't supposed to have been driving.

The sensible thing to do, he reasoned, was to skip school and play pool. He'd been doing a lot of it lately, anyhow, and now it seemed like he had a worthy reason for repeating that stunt. He stayed away from classes for three days. Just long enough for him to win the hundred he needed and a little extra. He had accomplished his mission. He had done what he had to do. He had acted honorably.

The dean didn't see it that way.

"Let me word it delicately," the frowning man said in the privacy of his office. "You better change your ways, kid, 'cause the next time you screw up, you're going to be expelled. Permanently."

Those words, coming from the usually mild-mannered dean shot right through Bobby's foggy arrogance. He didn't want to be kicked out. That would mean being sent to a special school for outcasts, separate from his friends.

"What's it going to be, Bobby?" the dean demanded. "You going to shape up, or am I going to ship you out of here?"

The dean's eyes were saying something. Bobby wasn't yet skilled in poker. But a primitive application of the talents he would one day develop told him the dean wasn't bluffing.

"I'm going to shape up," Bobby decided.

♠

I continued to shoot pool, but from that moment on, I got my act together: Not only did I put my grades back in order, I joined several clubs and devoted much of my time to formalized extracurricular activities. Throughout my junior year, I had only one chance to play poker. It was a six-handed dealer's choice game after school in a secluded corner of the gymnasium. Even though we felt pretty safe, snuggled between the side of the bleachers and the wall, I was a little jittery. The threat of expulsion still worried me. But nothing came of this illegal gambling experience on school property. The game lasted about forty-five minutes and died. I won a couple dollars.

It wasn't until summer vacation between eleventh and twelfth grades that I had any significant gambling experiences outside of pool.

That was the summer that Danny's parents bought him a car—a sparkling '64 Galaxie in perfect condition. Although he continued to throw off a good share of his money to me at pool, Danny and I had become best friends. So we planned a trip. Not just a drive into Kansas or down to Texas, but all the way to Los Angeles.

Neither of us had ever been to the West Coast. Steve and Charlie, present at my first poker experience, were also invited—plus a newcomer to our circle of friends named Pat. So we all said good-bye to our families and girlfriends (mine was now Debbie) and set off for the City of Angels.

♠

It was a pretty car, only two years old with a strong engine. In appreciation of this fact, the five took turns at the wheel. The accelerator spent most of the time pinned to the floorboard. In that year, very little of the distance was covered with divided highway. So there were a few close calls. Oncoming trucks left such a wind when passing that the boys feared their speeding Galaxie would be swept from the road. Once, an armadillo caused them a near tragedy. Charlie spun up a cloud of dust at ninety miles an hour avoiding the poor animal. For a second it looked as if Charlie would be unable to maneuver the car back from the road shoulder onto the asphalt.

Meanwhile, a poker game was in progress. Pulses raced for several minutes after the near disaster with the armadillo. But Pat dealt the cards shakily to himself and the three others crowded into the back seat.

They were playing a game that Pat, the youngest, had introduced. It was called Lowball. You play it like Five-Card Draw, except the lowest hand wins, with aces considered low and straights and flushes not counting against you. That meant 5 4 3 2 A was the best possible hand. And that was the hand that Bobby was dealt pat on the first deal after the near accident.

He played it cool. "Open for twenty cents," he said, placing two dimes into a paper plate on the floorboard.

The game had been going on for hours, four-handed with the boys taking turns driving. For the most part, the driving was pretty reckless. Too much so, from Bobby's point of view. Even though he tended to drive overly fast, he was definitely the most cautious of the five.

"Slow up a little, Charlie!" he advised, half out of concern that his dimes would shake out of the plate and half out of fear for his life.

"What's the matter? Afraid Charlie can't handle it?" Pat chided with moderately good humor. "Maybe you got a good hand or something. Well, I call."

In fact, they all called. After Bobby declared he wanted none, Pat drew one card, Steve three and Danny two.

Now Bobby bet a dime.

Pat was only fifteen and hadn't yet got his driver's license. Because of that, he felt a little less mature than the rest who, except for the eighteen-year-old Charlie, were all sixteen. The fact that he'd introduced the game of Draw Lowball to this group and the fact that they all liked it gave him a feeling of prestige. Somehow he felt it was he who was running the show.

So it was with a touch of authority that he said, "Seems like your hand ain't so good now that we're all drawing to beat it. Guess it ain't worth twenty cents no more, huh?"

Those natural talents that would some day make Bobby Baldwin the premier poker player in the world were spinning toward the surface of his brain. He sensed an opportunity. Acting mostly on instinct, he responded to Pat's ridicule by seizing the dime back from the paper plate.

In doing this, he had to be careful not to expose his hand, since the four of them were arranged in the back seat virtually along a straight line. There was sort of a "gentlemen's agreement" that, under these less-than-perfect conditions, no one would go out of his way to look at another's cards.

"I don't have such a weak hand! So I'll bet fifty cents, if that's what you want." Instead of the single dime, Bobby now bet two quarters. He had correctly registered the vibrations emanating from the younger Pat. Pat has a good hand, these vibrations said, otherwise he wouldn't have commented on my bet. If I act as if I'm intimidated by his words and bet more that he thinks I want to, then he'll feel obligated to raise more than he normally would.

It worked. Pat believed he had succeeded in goading Bobby into making an overlarge bet and immediately raised two dollars. Steve and Danny passed. Bobby—pretending to still be upset by Pat's earlier comments—threw in two dollars clumsily, but purposely let a third fall into the plate.

"You raising?" asked Pat sarcastically, certain that Bobby had intended to merely call.

"I put in two dollars," Baldwin said, feigning annoyance at Pat's question.

"You put in *three*," Pat corrected. "You wanna raise a dollar?"

Again Bobby appeared stunned when, in fact, he felt confident and in control. For the first time he was manipulating a poker player consciously, getting Pat to do exactly what was wanted of him.

"All right," Bobby conceded in a voice he tried to make irritable. "I raise a buck, then."

Pat jumped at the bait. "Okay, then I raise you ten bucks more."

Steve and Danny were watching intently. They had never seen this much money wagered in a poker game. When they'd agreed to play no-limit, they'd thought that the bets would remain reasonable. After all, they were only anteing a nickel. Even Charlie glanced back several times in the rear-view mirror and quizzed, "What's going on back there?"

Bobby quickly emptied his pockets. The pretending was over. Now the pot was so big that Pat would have to call. Bobby bet everything. Since he'd come with about forty dollars in his pocket, the amount of his raise was more than Pat could cover. Finally, Pat came up with twenty-one dollars. He called, only to find moments later that his 6 5 3 2 A, the third best possible hand in Lowball, was not nearly good enough.

Bobby agreed to lend the stunned younger boy whatever cash he needed during the remainder of the trip. It was getting dark. Already the headlights of their speeding car could be vaguely seen against the pavement. The game was suspended.

Later, I would learn to control my urges to overact. I'm a somewhat sedate poker player, not much of a performer. Many of the top professionals act like they're on stage whenever they sit in a poker game. Their routines are polished and perfect. I have nothing but the highest regard for these superstars of the poker world. You've got to admire their imagination,

their powers of perception, and their ability to manipulate other players in a game. You've got to respect their flare.

But that's not me.

Pretty much, I play the quiet style of my great friend Doyle Brunson, who won the world championship in 1976 and 1977. Occasionally, I'll use subtle persuasion to get called or to convince an opponent to lay down the better hand. In the world of top-level pro poker, elaborate gimmickry usually fails. Your opponents have seen it all before. They're wise to it. And if you use it too often, they're apt to get annoyed and find more congenial opponents for their next poker game.

Having said that, it still remains true that the stunt I pulled on Pat was a milestone in my poker career. Though I still knew little about appropriate card strategy and finesse, I had learned that an opponent could actually give his hand away while making an effort to conceal it.

That's a very important point: Most times you get a tell on a man, it's because he's making an extra powerful effort to make you think the opposite.

We continued racing toward Los Angeles through the night. Should we stop at a motel? We took a vote. Mine was "yes"—but it was three-to-two and I was on the losing end. The trip was 1,370 miles. During the night, a tire blew out. Steve was driving. We swerved all over the road, barely avoiding a truck. The driver stopped, and since we didn't have a spare, he took us up the road to a 24-hour gas station. We could get the nearly bald tire fixed or buy a replacement for $25. Another vote. This time I lost four-to-one. We stayed with the bald tire.

Around mid-morning we crossed the mountains and looked down into the L.A. basin. Lots of smog. Shortly after noon, we were in the city. It wasn't one single city, just a lot of suburbs bunched together endlessly. Finally we found a motel in Hollywood. It was called the Sahara, and since we knew there was a major casino by that name in Las Vegas, we felt this was an appropriate resting place for five adventuresome gamblers.

I slept until midnight.

HOLLYWOOD, CALIFORNIA
A SERIOUS GAME

Bobby was first to awaken. He'd slept through the day and it was midnight. He turned on the television at low volume, found nothing to his liking, took a shower and went looking for a soft drink machine. He found one in the office lobby.

A couple had just checked in, and the sleepy manager was preparing to return to his bedroom.

"You boys like the room?"

"It's fine."

"Well, there's a guy in the room next to you—been livin' there for two months—who's a little deaf. You know, he turns up the television real loud. He plays poker in Gardena most every night. Don't get home till sometimes four in the morning. So if he bothers you, just let me know."

"Where's Gardena?" Bobby asked, the mere mention of poker stimulating his curiosity.

"I'd say 'bout twenty minutes south down the freeway," the man yawned. "Why? Think you're a poker player?"

"Yeah, I play a little."

"Well, you gotta be twenty-one to get in. Besides, they don't play Seven-Stud or nothing like that. Only games legal are Five-Card Draw and Lowball."

"Lowball? I know how to play that."

"Speak of the devil! Here's the man I was telling you about. How'd you do tonight, Henry?"

Henry was a tall, slender man of about fifty-five, wearing tiny glasses that fitted his nose almost comically. He peered down at the young Baldwin, looking like a librarian scrutinizing a pesky child.

"What you say there, young 'un?" Henry greeted blandly.

"Nothing much," Baldwin said. "How 'bout you?"

The manager said, "You gotta speak up. He don't hear too good."

"Kid says he likes to play Lowball," the manager shouted.

Bobby and Henry walked back toward their rooms, leaving the manager to return to his dreams. "I got a deck and some chips," Henry said. "You can just come over if you feel like it. I'm right next door."

"Maybe. I'll have to see if any of my friends woke up yet. They might want to do something."

No one was awake. Bobby thought and thought. He'd never played cards with a stranger. He figured this situation called for caution. So cautiously he thought it over.

Then he barged headfirst into it.

When he knocked on Henry's door, his heart thudded. But the man put him at ease. In fact, it was Henry who insisted that both of them put up cash to buy chips. Baldwin wouldn't have to worry about getting paid.

Another reason he wouldn't have to worry about it was: he never got ahead. It just seemed that, although Henry drew two and three cards occasionally, Bobby was drawing more cards, more often. And not seeming to connect, to make it worse.

About twenty minutes into this one a.m. competition, Bobby finally made a miracle. He'd turned a three-card draw into a six-high and beat Henry out of four dollars. The next hand saw Bobby make a two-card seven. But it lost! Things got worse, and pretty soon Bobby had gone through more than thirty dollars and had no more in his pocket.

"Be right back."

Shaken by his bad fortune, the sixteen-year-old Baldwin returned to his own motel room and shook Danny out of his slumber.

"I need some money, Danny. Ten bucks will do."

"Okay. Just take it out of my pocket. Over there on the chair. What time is it anyway?"

Learning that he'd been sleeping roughly twelve hours, Danny got up, dressed and accompanied his friend to Henry's room. Things got a little better, then worse, then better. At least Bobby was holding his own, though. In truth, Henry was the superior player. Even Danny sensed that, but not Bobby. He just kept plowing into pot after pot with two card draws.

Until Bobby got stuck over forty dollars, they'd been playing dollar limit. Then Henry suggested they remove the limit and allow either player to bet whatever he could come up with, so long as the other guy could cover the bet. Playing that way, Bobby ran several successful bluffs and got to where he was only losing $23. The last hand they played went like this: Bobby holding K 5 3 2 A, opened for fifty cents. Henry raised two dollars, Bobby raised two dollars more, Henry raised five dollars and Bobby fought off an urge to raise again and decided to just call.

Henry dealt two cards to Bobby.

"One! I want one," Baldwin said.

"What?"

He half shouted, "You gave me two cards. I just want one."

"Oh," said the partially deaf man, sliding the second card back onto the top of the deck. "I don't want none."

Bobby was first to bet. He looked at his card, squeezing it secretly. A four! Bobby had made the perfect Lowball hand, a wheel. He bet ten dollars and Henry hesitated, looked back at his hand, considered raising, and finally just called. The showdown saw Bobby's wheel knock off Henry's 6 5 4 3 A.

Shaking his head miserably, Henry said, "You sure you got the right card? I gave you two and you only took one, so how d'you know you got the right 'un?"

"Well, you were dealing," Danny volunteered.

"What?"

"He said, you were the dealer," Bobby repeated loudly.

Henry thought it over. "I guess that's right. I reckon I'll just turn in now. I'm pretty darn tired. Lost sixty bucks tonight in Gardena. Thought you were going to help me out, young 'un, but you play a pretty good brand of poker."

Bobby accepted the compliment with a smile, although looking back on it years later, he realized that the man had been gracious. In any case, Bobby had lost only three dollars and the game was over.

CHAPTER 7

Ace-to-Five Lowball

The one thing Lowball does better than high-hand wins poker is generate excitement. I was really enthralled by the game the first time I played. Since all forms of Lowball require fewer strategies and less knowledge than high varieties, you can almost play automatically once you've learned the basics. But in my competition against Henry, I didn't even know those basics. I'd lost three dollars. And I'd been lucky.

COMMON MISTAKES

MISTAKE ONE:
Playing two-card draws from an early position

Novices tend to think of certain hands as playable and others as unplayable. Position is not one of their considerations. For this reason, you frequently see a player in second position making the mistake of drawing two cards to a bicycle when there are too many players waiting to act.

MISTAKE TWO:
Opening with a one-card draw to an 8 in the first three seats

If you don't have a one-card try for a seven or better in an early seat, you should pass.

MISTAKE THREE:
Laying down jacks, queens, and kings after the draw

Unsophisticated players tend to throw these hands away too frequently. Mathematical analysis suggests that a call is often reasonable when you've caught a face card and the bettor has also drawn. Otherwise, you'll find yourself bluffed out of too many pots.

MISTAKE FOUR:
Checking 9s and 10s in a draw-against-draw situation

When your opponent and you have both hit the deck, you should usually bet a 9 or 10.

MISTAKE FIVE:
In multiple blind games, playing too loose in the small blind

This is a recurring error for most beginners. In games that are open-blind, raise-blind, the small blind should not usually be defended against a raise.

MISTAKE SIX:
Breaking a 10 to draw to the worst hand

If your opponent has drawn cards, you should never break a 10 if you figure he's drawing better. However, if you think you'd be drawing to the better hand, or there's a good chance that you would be, it's often okay to break the 10 and try to improve.

MISTAKE SEVEN:
Assuming that 8 4 3 2 and 7 6 5 4 are about equal drawing hands

True, a pat 8-4 and a straight 7 are very nearly of the same value. But a one-card draw to a straight 7 is vastly superior to a one-card try at an 8-4.

FINAL FORMULA

RULE ONE:

Don't draw two cards from an early position.

RULE TWO:

You must have at least a one-card draw to a 7 in the first three seats.

RULE THREE:

If you and an opponent have both drawn, usually call if you don't pair.

RULE FOUR:

If you and an opponent have both drawn, bet a 9 or a 10 for value.

RULE FIVE:

Never break a pat 9 or 10 if you think you're drawing worse than your opponent.

RULE SIX:

Always break a 9 or 10 if you figure to have the better one-card draw.

RULE SEVEN:

After the draw, once an opponent has checked into you, don't try to bluff. Bluff mostly when you're first to act.

RULE EIGHT:

In an open-blind game, don't go crazy defending the blind. In a raise-blind game, don't overplay the small blind.

♠

Knowing none of these vital facts about Ace-to-Five Lowball, I had done poker combat with the hard-of-hearing Henry in a motel on Sunset Strip. It had cost me three dollars, but it should have cost a lot more.

For the next five days, we journeyed around southern California. Disneyland, the beaches. In motel rooms, I managed to rustle up two more poker games with my friends and won both times. I tried to talk the others into visiting Gardena, a suburb of L.A. which bills itself as "the poker capital of the world." None of the guys thought we'd be admitted, since you had to be twenty-one. So, to this day, I never have visited Gardena's card clubs.

Since I had a pocketful of money by the time our week-long vacation was over, I decided to fly back to Tulsa. Two things motivated me. First, I didn't relish driving back at 100 miles an hour on a bald tire. Second, my relationship with Debbie was a bit stormy. We seemed to get along sometimes, and at other times we had the most brutal arguments in the history of teen-age romance. I mean, it was just awesome the way we changed our attitudes about each other back and forth. Talk about a love-hate relationship. We had one. Even though we were steadies, I had the feeling that she might be tempted to date another guy while I was safely away in Los Angeles.

So, using my poker winnings, I caught a United flight to Tulsa in time to greet Debbie arriving home from a night out with one of our school's football elite. Thank God for poker!

♠

Bobby's relationship with Debbie stabilized. He continued to devote a lot of attention to school. His grades were mostly A's, and he was involved with several clubs. An all-girl club voted him their male mascot. It was an honor that most any guy in the senior class desired. You got to be with some of the prettiest girls on campus in situations where all other males were excluded. Additionally, he joined an all-boy club of which he was voted treasurer.

His ambitions for that latter club went beyond the ordinary. After several projects, garage sales, and car washes, Bobby's club had more money in its treasury than any other club at the high school. But this didn't satisfy the teenage Baldwin. They planned a Las Vegas Night where real money would be wagered on roulette, blackjack, and dice to win real prizes donated by local merchants.

"I can't let you do it, Bobby," said the kindly dean. It was Bobby's first confrontation with the man since he had almost been expelled during his sophomore year. "It's a question of legality. It could very well be against the law, even if all you can win is prizes. It's still gambling."

The dean paused ominously to let this last word sink in. Then, fearful that the whole import of the thing wasn't registering with Baldwin, he repeated in hardly more than a whisper, "Gambling. It's gambling, Bobby."

"Half of the profits are going to charity," Bobby said, even though the concept had never crossed his mind till that very second.

"Really? What charity?"

"Well, there's, ah . . . the people who are . . . old. Old people in wheel chairs." His words seemed to cement the idea in his own mind. Why shouldn't half their profits go to old people in need of assistance? People who couldn't get around normally? Seemed like a nice gesture.

"But it's gambling," the dean persisted stubbornly.

"But old people in wheel chairs need money."

The dean stammered, pounded the eraser end of his pencil rapidly on the desk and sighed.

Las Vegas Night was a big success.

Bobby's on-and-off infatuation with Debbie had jammed in the "on" position and was now a flaming romance. Not that they didn't get on each other's nerves. Something in their characters seemed to collide time and again. But for now, they clung to each other.

All during his senior year of high school, poker was in the background, pool in the foreground. In fact, he'd become so proficient at pool that he carried with him at all times more money than he could possibly spend. So, when he came up with an $800 down payment for a new car, his father Ken Baldwin agreed to go down to the dealership and sign the finance contract for the rest of it.

It was a close family. Often, thinking back on how he'd been drawn toward the gambling life, Bobby remembers a conversation he had with his father just weeks before that first poker game at Mark's. His dad was quitting his job, selling his luxury car, and taking a stripped down model without air conditioning.

"I'm going into business for myself, Bobby. Sometimes you've got to make sacrifices. Sometimes you've got to take chances. I hope you never have to spend you life working for someone else, not having full control of your own destiny."

They were words which clung to Bobby's mind. Words that drew him close to his dad whenever there were risks to be taken.

The business went slowly, then began to pay, then prospered. By the time that it did, Bobby was already so intrigued with pool and poker that it seemed inevitable that gambling would be a permanent part of his lifestyle.

There was a temporary rift in his romance with Debbie when she decided to go to Oklahoma University rather than Oklahoma State University, the college Bobby had chosen. O.U. was more of a partying, social school where you practically had to join a fraternity or sorority. As far as Bobby could ascertain, there were no regular poker games. O.S.U. was different. He knew of one game held every Thursday in the dorms. There was a more relaxed atmosphere, and he wouldn't be expected to join a fraternity.

Pool continued as a source of income for Bobby all through his freshman year. At O.U., Debbie found a new steady and her relationship with Bobby was temporarily interrupted. Meanwhile, his first session at the Thursday night poker game was a disaster. It was dollar-limit Seven-Stud, a game Bobby knew next to nothing about.

CHAPTER 8

Seven-Stud

I thought of myself as courageous, trying bluff after bluff. For some reason, my instincts were working. I could sense when the opponents were ready to fold. I made money on these bluffs, but I lost excessively by overplaying hands that were not the favorite. I just didn't have any minimum standards to fall back on. I was floating around, trying to figure out which hands were playable, which hands called for a raise, which hands should be thrown out.

If there's a truth that applies equally to all forms of poker, it's this: You must have minimum standards. Without them, you have to use 90% of your concentration deciding every time what to do with a given hand. All that mental energy should be devoted to studying your opponents and trying to decipher the small things that make this hand slightly different from similar hands you've seen in the past. You can act on those small differences, but only if you know for sure what it is you're supposed to do most of the time in that category of situations. So, never sit in a game without having a preconceived set of guidelines telling you what your minimum calling hands and raising hands should be. Then, once you can follow this set of standards automatically, look for reasons to make exceptions.

You'll find that a basic difference between a top-notch professional and a skilled amateur is that the pro spends just about all his time looking for exceptions. If he doesn't find reasons to vary his play from the basic plan, he sticks to that plan without wavering. But the point is, he can find more exceptions, he catches more tells, because he can afford to devote almost all his time to these more subtle areas of poker. He knows without conscious thought what hands he should normally play and how to play them.

As I was saying, I went into the first Seven-Stud game at the dorm without any set of standards, and they treated me none too kindly.

COMMON MISTAKES

MISTAKE ONE:
Trying to play a premium pair against a large field of opponents

Pairs of 10s, jacks, queens, kings and aces on the first three cards should ideally be played against a small number of opponents, preferably heads-up. For some reason, average players try to hide in the forest with these hands, letting as many players in the pot as possible and, consequently, often losing to straights and flushes.

MISTAKE TWO:
Playing come hands too aggressively

When you're trying for a straight or flush, you want to get the largest odds possible for your money. That means keeping players in the pot.

MISTAKE THREE:
Playing small pairs without taking the side-card into consideration

Anytime you begin with a pair less than tens, you're in a vulnerable position. Usually you need your third card to be bigger than the up-cards of other active players.

MISTAKE FOUR:
Playing small three-flushes and three-straights

These starting hands are almost always unplayable.

MISTAKE FIVE:
Not watching for key cards in other hands

Anytime you play a straight or a flush, you should pay particular attention to see how many useful cards are present in the hands of your opponents. Pass when you see a lot of cards you need.

Obviously the same sort of reasoning applies to situations where you begin with, say, a pair of fours. If you see another four out, you should almost never play.

MISTAKE SIX:
Continuing with an early bluff once it seems hopeless

It's okay—in fact it's desirable—to try to steal pots early in Seven-Stud, particularly if you think you can pick up an ante. But be ready to turn loose of the hand if things don't work out.

MISTAKE SEVEN:
Treating concealed pairs and split pairs alike

The unskilled Seven-Stud player doesn't recognize that two 8s in the hole with a 7 showing is much, much more potent than an 8 up with an 8 and a 7 in the hole. In the latter case, you have the hand your opponent will expect. In the first case, you have a powerful buried pair, and if you catch another 8, players will have no way to suspect you've made trips.

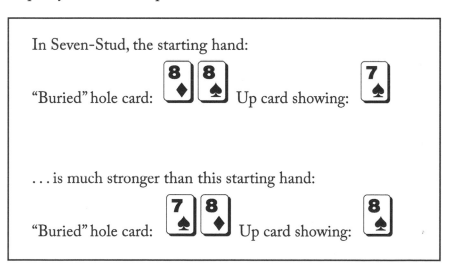

In Seven-Stud, the starting hand:

"Buried" hole card: 8♦ 8♠ Up card showing: 7♠

... is much stronger than this starting hand:

"Buried" hole card: 7♠ 8♦ Up card showing: 8♠

MISTAKE EIGHT:
Making routine laydowns on seventh street

Although, as a rule, weak Seven-Stud players tend to play too many hands, they also fold too often after seven cards against just one opponent. By then the pot is frequently offering 15-to-1-or-greater money odds, and often a call is almost mandatory unless your hand is totally hopeless.

FINAL FORMULA

RULE ONE:

When you begin with a pair of 10s through a pair of aces, try to eliminate players quickly.

RULE TWO:

With a drawing hand (three to a straight or flush) try to keep as many players in the pot as possible.

RULE THREE:

Generally, when you begin with three-of-a-kind, don't raise until the fifth card.

RULE FOUR:

Seldom begin with a small pair unless your side-card is larger than your opponents' up cards.

RULE FIVE:

Play concealed pairs more liberally than split pairs.

RULE SIX:

Don't play small three-flushes or three-straights.

RULE SEVEN:

Keep track of the cards in other players' hands.

RULE EIGHT:

After seven cards, usually call against a single opponent unless it seems hopeless.

RULE NINE:

Don't pay for a fifth card unless you're prepared to take a seventh card.

RULE TEN:

If three or more key cards are out, don't play for a straight or flush.

RULE ELEVEN:

If you get called trying to make an early steal, throw your hand away on the next bet. Give it up.

♠

Some of these concepts came to me during the next several sessions of poker. Others took years to sink in. Anyway, during my sophomore year at OSU, I was breaking about even at poker and piling up some heavy scores at pool. Where those guys got so much money to shoot pool with, I still don't know. But by midway through the first semester I had accumulated over five grand. Then the group of guys I played poker with got their heads together and decided to take a trip to Vegas. It was to be a junket, rooms and transportation paid by the Aladdin Hotel. As much as I wanted to see the big lights on the strip and the glitter of downtown, I had to decline. This was going to be a three-day vacation from classes, and I had promised my time to Debbie. (Yes, we were back together again.)

She sensed, though, that I was feeling pretty bad about missing my opportunity to visit Vegas. So, in good humor, she said, "Go win yourself some money. Really, it's okay. I want you to."

And I didn't argue. With a Kleenex box containing my $5,000 cash tucked into my suitcase, I boarded a plane. Las Vegas! The sound of the name rushed silently through my head. I was almost dizzy with *excitement. Already, at age nineteen, I thought of myself as a gambler. And here I was on an airplane that would soon land in a magic city devoted to my kind.*

♠

BOBBY BALDWIN: "Never play anyone soft."

CHAPTER 9

The Aladdin Hotel

LAS VEGAS (1970)

He was only nineteen and shouldn't have legally played in the casino. But no one asked for his I.D. and no one even scrutinized him closely.

Along on the junket was a friend of the family's from Tulsa named Bill. "The first thing you should do is go to the cage, ask for the manager and establish some credit." The mature Bill spoke this piece of advice as if it were an edict.

"I don't need credit," Bobby protested. "I brought five grand with me."

But Bill persisted. It was a good idea, he explained, to establish a line of credit. You never know when you're going to need it in the future, he argued. So, anxious to get into the serious business of gambling, Bobby walked with his friend through the busy casino to the cashier's window. With Bill's help, he quickly established $500 worth of credit.

Then Bill arranged for Bobby's complimentary room, plus a full refund on his airline ticket. *Great!* thought Bobby. *They treat you right in Vegas.*

He tipped the bellman a dollar for carrying the suitcase to his room. Then, alone, he unlocked his one piece of luggage and took out the Kleenex box stuffed with $5,000 worth of hundreds and twenties. He jammed about half of it into his pockets, not very neatly, and went briskly into the bathroom where he splashed water on his face. He was suddenly very eager and alert. Within a few minutes walk of this room was the dizzying, dazzling excitement of a major casino. People were down there winning and losing fortunes, he reminded himself. He strode briskly from the room, anxious to try his luck.

INITIATION

Several of his poker buddies were down in the casino gambling. Craps, blackjack, and roulette. Bobby, stifling an urge to barge right in, watched for a while.

He started shooting dice. It was a bad run. Occasionally, one of his pals from OSU would come by and give a sympathetic pat on the shoulders. But it just got worse. You couldn't tell night from day in the casino. Once Bobby walked out for fresh air, surprised to find the sky black above the commercial glitter of the strip, even more surprised to find it had been dark for three hours.

He returned to the craps game with renewed determination. But when the odds are fixed in favor of the house, determination won't do it. Courage won't make you win. Stubbornness doesn't help much, and you can't intimidate the house, no matter what. He lost, then lost some more, and by midnight he'd returned to his room twice for more money. By two a.m., despite a short-lived recovery during which he'd cut his losses to less than a grand, he had managed to burn up the entire $5,000.

When the final dice roll ate up Bobby's remaining fifty-five dollars, Bill said, "Let's go to bed. You can try again tomorrow."

Bobby declined, knowing that sleep would be impossible in the face of this savage tragedy. He got his $500 credit, courtesy of the Aladdin and shot some more. Bill hung around to watch the finish.

When Bobby was down to three green chips, worth $75, Bill again urged his younger friend to give up for the night. Bill thought he had some obligation to keep Bobby from going to bed completely broke. After all, Baldwin was the youngest member of the junket. He was the only one not legally old enough to enter the casino. It seemed reasonable that he needed some sympathetic protection and supervision.

"Well, hell," Bobby responded, "I might as well burn up this last seventy-five bucks. I'm broke anyway."

So Bill said, "All right. I'm going upstairs. See you tomorrow."

MIRACLE

On the next roll, Bobby thought *the hell with it.* He bet the whole $75. And won. Then he tested his luck with a $100 wager. That won. Next $150, and *that* won. A great excitement began to stir within him. When it was his turn to roll, he bet still bigger and threw the dice forcefully . . .

At 6:30 in the morning, he picked up the courtesy phone near the crap table. The phone in Bill's room rang six times before the older man answered.

"Yeah?"

"Bill, this is Bobby. Come on downstairs. I think I need you."

"What time is it?"

"I'll check . . . Bill, it's about six-thirty."

Bill hung up. Bobby rang his room again. Again Bill murmured sleepy, incoherent words and hung up. There were two security guards near the table. Bobby took two $25 green chips off his stacks and handed one to each guard. He scribbled Bill's name and room number on a piece of paper and handed it to the nearest one. "Could you please get this man out of bed and bring him down here?"

When Bill got downstairs ten minutes later, he looked at Bobby, then at the chips, and said, "I don't believe *this!*"

And Bobby said, "Well, neither do I, Bill. But they don't have any five-hundred dollar chips, so these are all hundreds. Can you help me cash in?"

Bill was monumentally excited. "Well, how did this happen?"

"I just took those three green chips and kept driving them. I guess I was lucky."

"Kid, if you only knew . . ."

When the chips were finally racked, hauled to the cashier's cage and counted, the final sum was $38,225.

Bill talked me into sending $30,000 back to Tulsa with a businessman—a friend of my dad's. I decided to stay the next two days of the junket. Even if I lost my remaining $8000, I'd be nearly a twenty-five grand winner for the trip. Well, I'd just never seen that kind of money before, and naturally, I was very excited over it.

The truth is, the incredible run of luck I had during my first visit to Vegas worked against me. I was a kid with little sophistication regarding the law of probability and the science of gambling. When you get lucky in the beginning, it just takes you that much longer to recognize the truth that you can't overcome fixed percentages and to discipline your gambling lifestyle.

I took a nap, a long one, and returned to the casino early that evening. While Bill was shooting dice, I ate dinner and goofed around, feeling euphoric about the way fate had treated me so far. Finally, after stalking the whole casino several times, I pounced on a blackjack table, buying five hundred-dollar chips.

Now, you've got to understand, I knew nothing about blackjack. The dealer had to show me how to stand and how to ask for a hit. I would hit fifteen when the dealer had a six showing. Sometimes I would stand pat with thirteen against a face card. There was just no consistency in the way I played. I had no set of standards. Obviously, I had no chance whatsoever of beating the game.

By six in the morning I had won $75,000.

I don't think anybody ever won as many hands in a short time as I did. I just about won every hand for a five or six hour stretch. It was just awesome. The most I ever bet was $500 a hand, playing three hands at a time. Still, there I was winning seventy-five grand without even knowing what I was doing.

THE ALADDIN HOTEL

It got to the point where I was having this guy who ran the junket fill $10,000 racks and take them to the window time after time. It was just too cumbersome having all those chips in front of me, particularly since they didn't have any of $500 denomination. He'd fill a rack and move it out, and I'd win more and he'd fill another rack and take that away. And when the smoke cleared, I was up $75,000. I was winning every hand, so I was going to play forever. I went to the men's room. Upon returning, I lost a couple hands. My interest waned. I quit.

We were going home the next day, and I wanted to get in some more action. I took a short nap.

The junket man rang my room at eleven in the morning and said, "Get up. Let's goof around and do something."

We went to the International and I played baccarat for about fifteen minutes. Knowing nothing about the game, I bet a straight $2,000 a hand. It didn't matter what I bet on, the bank or the player, I just won every hand. They kept saying strange words like, "Nine beats eight. Player wins." And whatever I was betting on, they just paid me. I won $50,000. A few hours later, we went to Caesar's Palace. Played baccarat again. Won another twenty-five or thirty thousand.

Before that morning rush, I'd called my dad in Tulsa and said, "You know Frank Neely?"

Dad said, "Of course, I do."

I said, "He's bringing home $30,000 that I won out here."

Dad didn't even know I was in Vegas, since I'd just taken off on the spur of the moment. All he could say was, "You know, that's great!"

The second time I called home, I said, "Dad, I got lucky. I've got about another hundred fifty thousand here that I've won." I told him that the junket man had worked out security for getting the money back to Tulsa. "Just meet me at the airport."

I'd never heard Dad sound so happy. "You won't have to work another day in your life," he told me.

♠

85

The same night, his parents were there to meet him at the Tulsa airport. "Here, Mom," said Bobby, handing the smiling woman a large narrow package, "I bought a dress for you."

She hugged her son tightly. "Thank you. Oh, Bobby, I'm so happy for you."

"I've got some business to take care of with Dad," said the younger Baldwin. "Take that on home. I'll see you in an hour or so."

Bobby's mother continued to praise him excitedly, but he secretly waved her away. "Can't talk right now," was all he said.

This espionage-like secrecy concerned Ken Baldwin somewhat, and he said, "Did everything go okay?"

"Yeah, fine. Had a plainclothes guard sitting three rows behind me on the flight. He carried a forty-five, so I felt pretty safe. See you."

An hour later, when Bobby reached the house, they had already discovered the money. Instead of a dress, Bobby had handed his mother a box full of cash.

"I thought it felt a little heavy," she beamed.

The three of them just stared at the money, scattered across the bedspread. None had ever seen money like this before. It was over $180,000. All three were almost childlike as they ran their hands through it and over it.

"Just take whatever you want," said Bobby. "It's yours just as much as it is mine."

Bobby and Ken decided the best bet was to invest $100,000 of the winnings, mostly in stocks. Since Bobby was now certain his destiny was to be a professional gambler, he kept $80,000 for his bankroll.

He only allowed himself one immediate luxury—an expensive set of poker chips engraved with his initials.

They were concerned about publicity, concerned about being robbed since it was Sunday and the banks were closed. These were objective fears, not merely fantasized paranoia. The next morning paper ran the story of Bobby's Vegas score, quoting $180,000 as the amount won and identifying Bobby Baldwin as the lucky junketeer.

It could mean trouble, and it did.

CHAPTER 10

Ominous Tidings

Except for Bobby's $80,000 gambling bankroll, which he divided and hid in six separate places, the Baldwin's got the money safely to the bank. Later that week it was invested, primarily in volatile stocks. The phone kept ringing, mostly strangers asking for money. Also, strangely, a rash of callers who hung up whenever anyone answered.

Beginning to think that his big score wasn't quite as terrific as he'd at first thought, Bobby returned to Vegas a week later on a second junket. He lost $25,000, perhaps a good thing because after that he was seldom eager to rush to Vegas and do battle with the house.

Other gambles continued. Already having lost about one-third of his bankroll, he began to take gin seriously. He got to be pretty good at it. Then some acquaintances set him up with a "cousin" from out of town.

"I've had enough," said Baldwin after losing about twenty-five grand.

"I'm real lucky tonight," said the cousin. "Maybe we can play again tomorrow."

"Yeah, okay."

"What time?"

The second session went the same way. The guy would go down with four points only if Bobby had more. When Bobby had just one or two points, the guy would wait for gin. For some reason, the stranger almost never discarded a helpful card. It was hopeless. Another twenty-five grand lost, and Bobby's bankroll was virtually gone.

Years later, Bobby learned that he'd been cheated. He'd been set up. The stranger, working in tandem with Bobby's acquaintances had used a peep hole in the ceiling to signal the out-of-towner what cards the young gambler was holding.

Stung by the two-month decimation of his bankroll, Baldwin tried to recoup his courage.

It was called the Bridge Club. More or less a social club, it was wedged between retail stores, part of a contiguous block-long shopping center. Besides bridge, there were games of gin and occasionally dominoes. Also, there was poker.

Here Bobby tried to get tough in his battle against a diminishing bankroll. He entered one day with his last twenty-eight hundred in his pocket and sat down to an afternoon of poker. It was Seven-Stud, and you could bet or raise anything up to the size of the pot, but the dealer could declare that they were either playing high-hand wins or low-hand-wins. Bobby had become pretty proficient at the high end, but this seven-card form of Lowball was new to him. Unfortunately, most of the hands dealt were Lowball.

When the end came, Bobby started out with a 4 exposed, a 3 and a deuce in the hole. Almost an ideal starting hand for Seven-Card Lowball. After several back-and-forth raises, only three players remained. Next card. Bobby caught a queen, and both opponents caught 7s. The man with the lowest hand, 7 with a 3, bet out and the 7 6 raised. Baldwin, no longer with the best hand, called the double raise, hoping the original bettor would not pop it again. No such luck! It cost Bobby two more sizable bets, each just under the sum of the pot in this pot-limit game.

By the seventh card, Bobby was all-in, third best and busted. Not only that, his dad had told him that morning that their stock investments had already lost 80%. The Las Vegas fantasy balloon had burst in Tulsa.

♠

You just can't imagine the pain. I looked back on it and thought, why? Those happy words of my father kept reverberating through my brain,

"You won't have to work another day in your life." Now I had blown it. I wasn't even twenty years old. And I felt terrible.

I remember so vividly scooting my chair back from the poker table and standing upright. "See you guys later," I said, and tried to smile. I still wonder if they knew—any of them—that now ninety days after my $180,000 win of a lifetime, I was totally broke.

No, I hadn't yet learned how to maintain a bankroll. I struggled just to fight off the pain. I felt like phoning Debbie at O.U. and telling her all about it. Someone's shoulder to cry on, you know. But, no, I decided. Besides, I hadn't even informed her of the big score I'd had in Vegas. She never asked me how I did, and I never told her. Due to some strange quirk of fortune, she never learned of the newspaper article heralding my lucky three days in the city of glitter. Why did I never tell her? I don't know . . . in spite of the closeness we felt for each other in most respects, she never seemed comfortable knowing about my gambling business. She was a good woman, but she wasn't a gambler's woman. Later I'd learn the difference.

About the poker game at the bridge club . . . I played poorly. Again I was just blundering around trying to guess at the right strategies. Again I was in a game without any pre-established standards. Which Seven-Card Lowball hands should I play? I didn't know. Which should I throw away? Beats me! No, I didn't win that day. Honestly, I wasn't supposed to win.

CHAPTER 11

Seven-Stud Lowball

COMMON MISTAKES

MISTAKE ONE:
Beginning with a picture card

Except in circumstances where other likely opponents also have face cards, you should never enter a hand with two baby cards and a picture. It simply isn't profitable.

MISTAKE TWO:
Trying to outguess an opponent on seventh street

Unless it looks totally hopeless, limit Seven-Stud Lowball strategy dictates that you usually should call a bet after seven cards. That's because there's usually enough money in the pot by then to justify a call in a straight-limit game. This, of course, is not true in those rare pot-limit (or no-limit) Seven-Stud low games, like the one I played at the Bridge Club.

MISTAKE THREE:
Failure to recognize that a smooth come hand is the favorite against a completed 9 after five cards

Example: K 5 3 2 A is the favorite to beat 9 8 7 6 3. The come hand, in this case, should be the aggressor, but usually isn't.

MISTAKE FOUR:
Never value betting after seven cards

You should always value bet a 9 into a player who appears to have a 10 made and is trying for a better hand. That's because you're going to get called by the 10. But be prepared to pass if you get raised.

MISTAKE FIVE:
Not playing a quality come hand after five cards aggressively in a multi-way pot

Your Q 4 3 2 A against one hand showing 9 2 A and another with 8 7 4 should be played as fast as possible. That means, raise if you're bet into.

MISTAKE SIX:
Not paying attention to what cards have been thrown away

Exposed cards are critically important. If you begin with A 2 3 and see a lot of 2s, 3s, and aces, you're in much better shape than if you're surrounded by 4s, 5s, and 6s—cards you need.

FINAL FORMULA

RULE ONE:

Against a strong-appearing board, don't start with a worse hand than 7 6 5.

"Buried" hole cards… Up card showing…

Seven-Stud Lowball: This starting hand is usually unplayable when opponents are betting small cards against you.

RULE TWO:

Against a single opponent, usually call on seventh street.

RULE THREE:

If a player gives you a lot of action on the first three cards, then catches a 7 or an 8, figure it did *not* pair him.

RULE FOUR:

If you and an opponent enter a pot with small up-cards and you catch a pair or a paint (meaning a king, a queen, or a jack) on fourth street while he snags a non-pairing baby card, you should fold.

RULE FIVE:

Play a smooth come hand after five cards aggressively against a rough completed 9.

RULE SIX:

Play a completed 8 after five cards very aggressively against *any* drawing hand.

RULE SEVEN:

Remember what cards have been folded and call, pass, or raise while taking this information into consideration.

RULE EIGHT:

In a three-or-more-handed pot, usually play very fast with a quality come hand.

CHAPTER 12

From Bad to Worse

At the urging of Dad and Bill Hickle—the family friend who'd been on my first junket to Vegas—I joined the country club. Dad was a golfer. Bill's basic interest at the country club was gin rummy. He and I played on several occasions. But, having exhausted my bankroll, the stakes were low. Nonetheless, I got on a rush, beating Bill and other club members pretty consistently for about a week. The size of the wagering grew from tiny to medium. And the size of my bankroll grew from nonexistent to small.

Then Bill introduced me to a gin rummy addict whose play was mediocre. I won almost $10,000 in four hours. Later that day, I stood in an automobile showroom admiring a new car.

I guess the salesman thought I had no business there, because he said, almost sarcastically, "Can I help you with something?"

And I said, "Well, I want to buy this car. How much is it?"

"Forty-eight hundred and sixty-three bucks," the man said blandly. "Excuse me, I have some papers to fill out." He just started walking toward the office.

"Well, will you take cash?" I said and began counting through a wad of hundreds I'd shoved into my pocket when I left the country club. I drove the car right out of the showroom that day, having sliced my brand new bankroll in half.

Contrary to public conceptions, some professional gamblers keep a low profile. Not me. I like the trappings that go along with the gambling lifestyle. I like fancy cars, fine clothes, and expensive houses. It's part of the dream.

My stretch of luck at gin ended. Three days later I was broke again, but at least I owned the car.

THE IRS WAS THE LEAST OF HIS CONCERNS

Things got very bad. The IRS wanted taxes on the $180,000 Bobby had purportedly won. Well, he didn't have the winnings any more. They were persistent; Bobby was persistent. Eventually, they settled for roughly $3,500 in taxes. It was clearly a rip-off from Bobby's viewpoint. After all, he'd lost back nearly 100% of the money gambling.

But the tax issue was not his foremost worry.

His money situation was somewhat worse than when he'd embarked on the Las Vegas adventure. He no longer had the five grand bankroll he'd started with.

He dropped out of school, electing to concentrate on a gambling career, bankroll or no bankroll. He scratched together a few hundred dollars, played a little pool and won. Played a little poker and won. Played gin and won. Nothing major, but he managed to put together a starting bankroll of just under $10,000.

He didn't let on that he'd blown most of his winnings. He *acted* like a man with a large bankroll. It was his style.

The man who ran the poker game at the Bridge Club introduced him to a newcomer named Rick. They became friendly, played an hour or so of gin, broke about even.

"Wanna walk across the street for a quick drink?" the man asked. "Don't figure I can play another hand without a cold beer."

Bobby shrugged his shoulders. Why not?

"She's something else," Bobby said wistfully, watching the waitress who had just gone to get their beers.

"Sure is," the new friend agreed. "Her name's Linda, and I can tell she's got the eye for you. Want me to set you up?"

"Just like that?"

"Yeah, sure. I come in here a couple times a week. Linda and me are good friends. Hey, Linda, come here."

"Just a second," she called back, smiling sexily, "I'm bringing your beers."

It sure went easy, Bobby thought as he and his new pal walked back to the Bridge Club. *She likes me. Pick her up at the bar at nine. Just like that!*

Gin went back and forth and ended with Bobby ten dollars on the winning side. "Keep it," he said. "For setting me up with Linda."

At seven that night, Bobby was playing poker at the Bridge Club when he was called to the telephone.

The unidentified man on the other end said, "Listen good. Can't talk long. You got a date tonight. Don't go."

"Well, I just . . ." Bobby began thinking, of course, that this was an irate call from a husband or boyfriend.

The voice cut him short. "It's a set up, Bobby. They're out to kidnap you. Don't comment, just say, 'That's fine' and meet me tomorrow at the Fairview Liquor Store, ten in the morning."

"That's fine."

"There's a couple of guys out to cause you some trouble. Just take my word for it. Cash out and go home." The man hung up.

Bobby did as instructed. Cashed out, went home, didn't bother to call and cancel his date. Linda was the first attractive female he'd ever stood up.

MEETING THE NEXT DAY

He was a man of about fifty. It was drizzling that day, and he stood with his rain coat hunched about his shoulders, water streaking down his face.

"Guess I should have brought my umbrella," he said pleasantly, but his face remained serious. It was ten a.m. sharp. "Walk around the corner of the building, Bobby. Don't want anyone to see us together."

The guy looked somewhat familiar. Then Bobby remembered. An occasional player at the Bridge Club. Gin, never poker.

"Can't tell you how I know. But I can't sit by and let you get hurt. Listen carefully. It comes down the grapevine, see, but it's dead on target, so you take heed. Got it? Not giving any names, either, but listen. Two guys are out to get you. Kidnap you and get a big ransom from your folks. Mean mothers, both of them. They're real serious about it, too. So this is my advice, listen good. Quit playing at the Bridge Club. Keep low, out of sight. Move away from your folks. Get yourself a place somewhere and don't tell a soul where it is, except your family. Gotta go, son, see you around."

A TALK WITH MOM AND DAD

"Oh, Bobby," wailed his alarmed mother. "What should we do?"

"Don't do anything, Mom. We've all got to agree on this. There's not going to be a ransom. You have to decide that now."

The three of them talked, virtually argued at times. But in the end Bobby convinced his parents that paying a ransom would not help to bring him home safely should the worst happen.

It was an emotional good-bye. He took an apartment near Tulsa University—in an older, crime-ridden area. It was a tiny, two-bedroom unit, but no one knew him there. He took on a roommate, a college student who'd been a friend of his since high school. Swearing the roommate to secrecy, Bobby explained the circumstances.

Bobby was taking no chances. He bought a big-caliber pistol and an attack-trained German Shepherd.

Every other night, Baldwin would attend a poker game in Brookside. The stakes weren't as large as the games at the Bridge Club, but Bobby was able to beat that gathering almost every play. He was, for the first time, developing professional-level poker skills. One night his roommate called him at the game in Brookside.

He'd been playing detective, he told Bobby. "And I spotted this car down the street with two men in it."

"What's wrong?"

"Maybe nothing. It's just been sitting there, a brand new Pontiac. Doesn't seem to fit in this dump of a neighborhood."

"I don't know, Connally, it could be any—"

"But, listen to this: I walk out there with Snarler on a leash, we start toward their car and they drive off real quick, like they don't want to be spotted."

"I still don't know. You might speed away yourself if Snarler was coming toward you," Baldwin pointed out.

"Anyway, I got the license number."

When Bobby had a hotel security guard check the number, it turned out that the car belonged to a woman in nearby Boroughsville. Bobby decided that the strange car did not portend great danger. Two nights later, someone smashed a window at their apartment. Looked as if the invaders got about halfway in and then, scared off by the vicious Snarler, retreated. The mangled Venetian blinds told the story.

So, quickly, Bobby moved into another apartment with another friend of his across town. Days passed, and he regained some sense of security. A shadow of safety enveloped him. He hadn't played poker for days. On impulse, he decided to risk a visit to the Bridge Club. It was afternoon, the sun was bright, and he had every intention of leaving before nightfall.

Bobby was playing his third hand of draw poker and had just made a correct laydown of three 7s when the man who had warned him of the kidnap plot entered the club. He cast Bobby a glance of surprise, then shrugged his shoulders and looked quickly away. Baldwin decided to sneak a talk with the man somehow, to thank him for his concern. Also, he would try to convince the man it was safe to divulge more information about the whole scheme. Yes, today they would have a critical talk. But by the time two more poker hands were dealt, the guy was already in a gin game with another patron.

Roughly a dozen hands later, a vigorous argument exploded between Bobby's informer and his gin rummy opponent. "You can't thumb through the discards!" shouted Bobby's mysterious ally.

"Whatcha talking about? Everyone does it!"

"Leave the discards alone, damn it!" Suddenly the informer made a groan. He struggled for breath, and in doing so he made an unearthly sound. Everyone turned to watch. He brought his hand flat against his chest and looked piteously about for help. He tried several times to catch his breath. More strange sounds flowed from deep within him. Without even trying to break the fall with his arms, he crashed to the floor and died.

"Oh, Christ!" said Bobby, rushing to the man's side. Another patron, tried to revive the man with Bobby assisting. Nothing worked. The man was gone. And so was Bobby's link to the kidnappers...

For a whole month, Bobby stayed completely away from the Bridge Club. Laid low, shot some pool. Finally, he got to where he couldn't stand it. He parked his car in a supermarket lot, and, without telling anyone he was coming, took a cab to the club. He figured if they didn't see his car parked outside, and had no way of anticipating his arrival, his visit was safe.

This reasoning was wrong.

CHAPTER 13

Where's Bobby?

A compulsive gambler is a person who uses gaming as a narcotic. More than just needing to be in action, he has an emotional need to lose. That's a fine distinction, but one worthy of noting. At that young age, I felt a powerful urge to be in action, to gamble. It was hard for me to turn down any opportunity. But the thing that kept my near-addiction from reaching the compulsive stage was my drive to win. I was downright stubborn. Sure, I seemed to habitually find myself in situations where I had the worst of it, but there were times, too, when the odds played overwhelmingly in my favor. No matter what the case was, my whole being cried out for victory. I never treated gambling as a form of self-punishment. Not consciously. That was always in my favor.

But we all have destructive urges. Seem like a reckless statement? It isn't. It's part of man's nature to stand stubborn in the face of challenge. And many of us feel compelled to create challenges whenever none present themselves. This is not wholly unhealthy. In fact all champions share this trait. A person who skydives is tempting fate. He earns the exhilaration of feeling alive.

But his activity is only healthy if the subconscious payoff is survival and not death. We must learn to modify our flirtations with danger. Our psyches must be geared to dueling with fate while assuring ourselves that we have the best of it. When you learn to do this, you possess the temperament of a winning gambler. Challenge fate at every turn without modifying these destructive urges and, sooner or later, you will destroy yourself.

To be successful in the art of gambling, you must recognize that you have destructive urges, but you must treat these as a life motivating force to be controlled by you. The willingness to court danger— to jeopardize life or bankroll—is admirable. But the undisciplined surrender to those compulsions can be terminal.

By returning to the Bridge Club under dangerous circumstances, I wasn't using mature judgment. I had not yet learned to weigh probable gain against possible loss and decide, on that basis, whether or not to take chances.

♠

Seven-Stud was the game that night. He had mastered many of the finesses and applied a comprehensive set of minimum calling and raising standards. But his luck was terrible. By the time the game broke up at eleven, almost an hour earlier than usual, Bobby was losing all but $700 of his bankroll. Then Bill Hickle suggested they play heads-up. The game was Ace-to-Five Lowball. For about an hour they stayed almost even.

In fact, they were *exactly* even when at three minutes till midnight, they agreed to one last hand of showdown for $718—everything Bobby had remaining. Bobby began to deal, a 6 to himself, a 4 to Bill. A jack for himself, a 10 for Bill, then a deuce . . .

Startled by a sudden crashing sound of metal on metal, Bobby leapt from the table and headed for the rear exit. It was a sound he'd been dreading in his imagination. Again the clang. An axe was colliding viciously with the steel door and the metal bolt that secured it.

The whole building seemed to shake.

There were now only a dozen members in the club, eleven males and the girl friend of Bill Hickle. A murmur of apprehension echoed though the room. Was this a raid or what? The woman grabbed Bill's arm for security, while most of the men hurried toward the back of the building away from the axe.

Bobby went out the rear, urging the others to follow. *It's not a police raid,* he worried. *It's the kidnappers!* Instinct told him this beyond any doubt whatsoever.

He was into the cold of night now, running along the alley. Just as he cleared the back door of the Bridge Club, gun shots powered their way though the exit. Bobby looked around. His silhouette was against the half open rear door. Bullets had pierced his shadow!

He hurried across the alley. There were back yards and a lot of trees. He worked his way between these, heading toward a cross street. But there was a long way to go. Someone rushed out of the rear of the Bridge Club. It was a guy who sometimes dealt the poker game, and he ran down the alley away from where Bobby hugged a too-slender elm tree. Could the kidnappers see Bobby there?

He chanced being spotted and ran deeper into a back yard, then veered across several lawns, increasing the distance between him and the club.

He thought he heard someone coming down the alley. Maybe it was just the wind teasing the trash cans. He ran. His foot collided with the exposed root of a tree. He crashed to the grass, rose almost without hesitation. He was like an animal, motivated by instinct— running, needing a place to hide.

Parked twenty yards ahead in the alley was a sports car. Dashing in its direction, he looked over his shoulder. No one. Only the chilly blackness of an empty alley, broken by a slice of light streaming from the partially opened back door of the Bridge Club. Then appeared a masked figure spotlighted within that thin piece of whiteness. Bullets cracked off one by one, and Bobby could see the muzzle flashes, the strange combination of artificial light against shadow causing a bizarre blend of powder white and blazing orange.

He reached the sports car and wedged himself beneath it. Not an easy thing to do. The frame was so close to the ground that Bobby tore his ear getting under it. The car had recently been driven, and the heat of the exhaust pipe brought pain against his shoulder. He remained still, his heart thudding. He listened. Voices came from inside the club, but it was too far away to make out what was happening.

Deciding not to follow Bobby out the exit, Bill and his woman had hid in the bathroom. There was a laundry hamper near the rear exit. One man jumped into it head first, but his feet hung over the top ridge, making it easy for anyone to spot him.

There were two of them, wearing ski masks. As soon as the bolt gave way, they thrust themselves through the front door. Seeing Baldwin leave, but not knowing who it was, the bigger man fired several times at the rear exit.

"Nobody move," barked the larger of the two men. He dropped the axe to the floor and pointed a black pistol toward the men gathered near the poker table.

"We're going to kill anyone who don't cooperate. Do what we say and you won't get hurt." That man seemed rational, in control.

But his buddy was crazed with drugs, shaking as he held his gun. He'd point first at one patron, then at another. "We might just kill you no matter what!" he shouted. Then he laughed, a hideous sort of laugh that chilled everyone. His sanity was in question.

The man who remained more in control said, "Go see who got out the back." The crazy one hurried to the rear entrance. Within several seconds the room resounded with gun shots fired into the alley.

"He got away!" shrieked the deranged kidnapper, waving his gun angrily as he returned to the Bridge Club interior. "That son of a bitch Bobby got away! That kid got out the back door. He got away! He got away! Jesus, he got away!" Then he kicked a wooden chair across the room. It crashed against the front wall.

They made everyone lie face down on the floor, emptying pockets, taking money, jewelry, credit cards, anything.

Paul was a regular, player in the poker game. When the crazy one said, "Give me your money," he handed over a wallet containing five dollars.

"This guy's only got five bucks!" the wild one raged. "Guess I better kill the sucker!" And without another word, he put his pistol to the back of Paul's skull and shot through his brain.

WHERE'S BOBBY?

♠

It seemed like forever. I just stayed underneath the sports car until I heard a siren. I began to dislodge myself from my uncomfortable position, wedged between the ground and the tailpipe. But the siren faded. It was only a passing ambulance.

More sirens. The police had finally arrived. In truth, it had been a very short time. A newspaper boy had seen the men in ski masks carrying an axe toward the front door and had tipped the police. They arrived about five minutes after the first swing of the axe against the metal entrance. Felt like a year, though.

I walked back up the alley, keeping pretty much toward the trees. A police cruiser squealed around the corner with its lights off and parked by the Bridge Club's rear exit.

"What are you doing here?" he asked when he spotted me. He didn't even have his gun drawn.

"I was inside when they broke in. I think it's me they were after because . . ."

The cop wasn't paying any attention. He just walked toward the rear door. Shots sounded as he started to enter. His knees buckled and he kind of bunny hopped backward, all the while trying to get his gun out of its holster. He stumbled into the trash cans, still trying in his nervousness to free his revolver.

He'd strode right up to the back door like he was John Wayne a few seconds before. As soon as the gun went off inside, he was about four feet tall, clumsy as hell and scared to death.

I thought, "Oh, Lord, I'm in trouble," expecting the kidnappers to barge out the back door at any moment. I could visualize this cop on his knees pleading for mercy while his gun remained jammed in the holster. Finally, he got lucky and the gun worked free.

Another cop car arrived, and soon I was crouching behind a squad car with an officer on each side. I could hear the cops in front bellowing on loud speakers, "Surrender. This is the police. Come out unarmed, hands up. Surrender."

That's when two silhouettes appeared in a darkened corner just inside the rear door.

"Stop!" yelled the officer to my right.

The bandits froze.

The crazy one said, "Okay, man, I've had it," and threw his gun into a trash barrel. His accomplice didn't do a thing. Now we could make them out more clearly. The one who still held a gun was only about five-eight, but a big, husky dude over two hundred pounds. The crazy one was a bit taller and very slender. Both still wore their ski masks.

Suddenly the drugged-up guy wheeled around and headed for the front door. He had another gun on him. (Each man carried a second gun.) He crashed through the front door waving a pistol insanely. They shot him all to pieces. All kinds of gunfire was going on up front, and during this commotion the dude who'd been standing by the back door jumped into the alley and started running.

"Stop! I'll shoot!" cried one cop, while the other echoed those words almost exactly.

Heedless of this warning, the man kept running. He turned back and fired a shot which hit the police car near where we were huddled low for protection. They opened fire on him. He dropped his gun right in the alley and continued running. He was so hefty for a guy his height that it just looked like he was running in slow motion. You could hear the bullets ricocheting off the concrete buildings and the asphalt of the alley. They fired until they were both clicking . . . used all six shots in both guns and never hit this guy. They just never hit him! He got down the alley, around the corner and out of sight.

During the commotion, I made my way back to the front of the shopping center. I found the guy who'd escaped down the alley in the other direction when the kidnappers had come through the front door.

He said, "Well, I guess we ought to go back over there and tell them our stories."

And I said, "Yeah, I'm sure glad to see you're all right."

"I'm glad to see you're all right, too."

We didn't know at that time what had happened inside, whether anyone was hurt or what. By then the police had all the spectators roped off.

"You can't go through," a cop said sternly.

But this woman friend of Bill's comes charging out of the club yelling, "There's Bobby! There's Bobby!" Apparently they'd been really worried about me.

There was blood everywhere inside the Bridge Club. Paul was unconscious, still lying on the floor where they'd put a bullet into his brain. An ambulance was just now arriving. There were bullet holes in the walls. The crazy guy lay dying out front. Because Paul had handed the man a wallet containing only five dollars, he'd been shot through the skull. Undetected was the more than $1,000 cash he had in a front pocket. Seemed like poor judgment on Paul's part.

Bill and his girl friend had escaped notice in the bathroom. Even more incredible, the guy who'd tried to hide himself headfirst in the hamper, while his feet stuck straight up in plain view, was undiscovered by the would-be kidnappers.

The police took us all to the station for questioning. They kept me separately. Apparently the drugged-up man kept saying, incoherently while he died, "That goddamn, Bobby! That goddamn kid!" Instead of interpreting this correctly as evidence that it was me the outlaws were after, the cops suspected I was in on the arrangement and had botched it. Things didn't get any better when I tried to explain about the $180,000 I'd won in Vegas and about the kidnap plot and the informer who'd died.

Finally, my folks provided them with a newspaper clipping, and we got it straightened out. The car my roommate got the license number on? It belonged to the madman's sister.

By the time I left the police station, they had captured the other kidnapper, a former cop gone bad. It required a pack of dogs. They found him lying face down in a field. Just wasn't anywhere to go.

What happened to my $718 that was on the table for the showdown hand with Bill? The police confiscated it. And since I couldn't prove it was mine without admitting to the criminal act of having gambled, they just used it for the most logical thing they could think of. It went to pay the attorney fees for the surviving kidnapper.

Thus disappeared the last of my bankroll, but the guy got a good lawyer.

CHAPTER 14

Five-Card Draw

Reality was rude to Bobby. In the aftermath of the shootout, he returned to Las Vegas, the fantasy land where he had walked away with almost two hundred grand not many months before. But he no longer had any meaningful bankroll. They weren't hostile toward him at the Aladdin. But they weren't very friendly. He'd been treated in princely fashion during his last visit. This time he couldn't get a complementary room—no food, no credit. He just wasn't welcome.

Pool and gin were definitely secondary to poker. It was poker that was drawing him toward his destiny. He could feel it, feel it surrounding him. Poker was becoming part of him, and he was becoming part of poker. By now, he already identified himself that way in his own mind—as a poker player. And he began to take the game very seriously.

He even started to do a bit of traveling, frequenting private poker games within roughly fifty miles of Tulsa. Muskogee, Bartlesville, Cashing—these were all sites of recurring home games to which Bobby found himself invited. Slowly, steadily, he began to rebuild his bankroll.

WICHITA, KANSAS

It was the first time Bobby had ever left his hometown specifically to play poker. A friend of the man who hosted the Muskogee game had invited him up to a game in Wichita. He'd agreed to "try to make it," although he felt pretty doubtful, since it was a rather long drive. Nonetheless, about noon on Friday, the urge struck him, and he arrived in Wichita in time for the game that evening.

Draw poker was the game this group played. Bobby knew only the basics, but during the drive, he formulated a set of guidelines that seemed reasonable. And he stuck to them almost a hundred percent.

Perhaps, he'd just guessed luckily, but the standards he adopted that night were effective. This was a friendly atmosphere: A comfortable farm-style home. Eight handed. Stakes moderate. Those stakes began at $2 limit, but ending up $5 limit by two in the morning—the pre-arranged cutoff time.

At about ten-thirty, a carpenter named Ed went busted. He smiled and said, "You're one hell of a player, Mr. Baldwin."

The host's brother-in-law went all-in against Bobby an hour later. After losing, the man graciously said, "I wish I could comprehend your style of poker, son. Every time I throw my hand away, you're bluffing. Every time you've got the goods, I call. Well, it's been a pleasure playing with you." They shook hands.

Bobby broke two more of the participants. When the game concluded, it was only four handed. Bobby had won over four hundred dollars.

The man who had invited him to the game took the much younger Baldwin aside. "Maybe you could give me a few pointers so I can be more competition for you next time you drive up."

Bobby beamed. It was the first time anyone had ever asked for his advice on poker.

Bobby at the table with Amarillo Slim in the audience

COMMON MISTAKES

MISTAKE ONE:
Playing open-end straight draws

In a limit game of draw poker, there is almost no justification for ever drawing to these "country" straights. A hand like K 9 8 7 6 is just about always unplayable.

MISTAKE TWO:
Opening in an early position with two small pair

It doesn't matter whether the game is jacks-or-better to open (a common form of draw) or guts, meaning anything can be used to open, and it doesn't matter whether you're playing with or without the joker—opening with 10s and 6s with five or more players is to act

113

suicidal. You can't call a raise, and therefore your hand is vulnerable. It's much, much better to check and see if someone else opens. Then, either call, raise, or pass when the action gets back around to you.

MISTAKE THREE:
Not opening with aces

Always open with aces unless there's a clear-cut reason for checking.

MISTAKE FOUR:
Keeping an ace kicker against a two-card draw

If your opponent has three-of-a-kind, you certainly want to draw three cards to a pair of kings, giving yourself a better shot at beating his trips. If he, too, is holding an ace kicker, your chances of catching an ace are diminished and you definitely ought to draw three.

MISTAKE FIVE:
Calling an opener in a jacks-or-better game with kings

Unless you *know* your opponent has less than aces, you *must* pass.

MISTAKE SIX:
Calling a pat hand with three-of-a-kind

Silly as it seems, a great many players have a policy of never laying down trips. It's a mistake of gigantic financial proportions.

FINAL FORMULA
RULE ONE:

Unless there are two active players in front of you, never play a 4-flush.

RULE TWO:

Never draw to an open-end straight.

RULE THREE:

Don't open early with any two pair smaller than aces-up.

RULE FOUR:

Always open with a pair of aces.

RULE FIVE:

Keep a kicker only when there's an obvious reason for doing so. When in doubt, draw three to a pair, two to three-of-a-kind.

RULE SIX:

Never call an opener in a jacks-or-better game with less than aces.

RULE SEVEN:

Be prepared to usually throw away three-of-a-kind against a pat hand.

CHAPTER 15

A Gambler's Woman

One thing was certain: Debbie didn't like gambling. Not when he won, not when he lost. Their natures were different. Her paradise was comfort and security. His was challenge and adventure. Still, there was some intangible magnetism that inevitably captured them.

After a few years of traveling in a small poker circuit around Tulsa, gaining skills and a winning a reputation, he married Debbie.

Because she needed the emotional security of knowing he held a steady job, he began working part-time at his father's construction business. Mostly, though, he devoted his energy to poker.

They blundered through the marriage day by day, but soon the friction outweighed the comfort and they agreed to a divorce. After six months the divorce became final. Sort of.

They rekindled the emotional warmth they had previously shared.

"I suppose you want to try again?" she asked coyly, hoping that his response would be affirmative

"Well, maybe that's what we ought to do," he said. "But I don't see how it's going to work much better this time, Debbie."

"Bobby, I just don't see how it will, either."

"Then it's almost hopeless," Bobby said.

"Hopeless," Debbie echoed.

Having agreed on something for a change, they felt it was only fair to give their relationship another chance. The judge was understanding. Even though the divorce was technically final, since the six month waiting period was over, his Honor decided that they could consider themselves still married.

Bobby began to bet football. It was an expensive decision. Coupled with a bad run at poker, his bankroll dropped to under $40,000 for the first time in nearly a year.

Debbie said, "Bobby, I just can't take this way of life—you being on the road. You go off to poker games, and sometimes I don't even know when you'll be back. I want you to settle down. I mean it."

Well, this was just the sort of talk that always upset Baldwin. "I'll say it one more time, Debbie. Gambling is my life. It's the way I am, the way I want to be, the way I always *will* be. There'll be good times and bad times and you'll never know from day to day which it's going to be. If you can't handle it, maybe you should just move out."

They were daring words, Bobby thought. Perhaps once and for all he could silence her criticism of his lifestyle. Maybe now, finally, she would get it through her head just how serious he was about gambling. Maybe now they could stop the bickering, settle back and enjoy each other peacefully.

He didn't even wait for her response. "I'll be back in a couple hours," he said, enjoying the feeling that he had acted decisively with Debbie. The mild-mannered young gambler had spoken. He shut the door quietly as he left.

She had cleaned everything out. *Everything.* All her belongings were gone. She had taken lamps, furniture, photographs. All that remained were his clothes. He went though the kitchen drawers. Empty. And then, lying in plain view in the drawer where the silverware used to be, he found a bent spoon. It had been mangled in the garbage disposal. He shrugged his shoulders and said aloud, "Guess she didn't have any use for it."

He bummed a beer from the apartment next door. Then he sat on his balcony sipping the brew and thinking. Between his fingers, he played with the twisted spoon. The sun was setting and the last light of day glared against the silvery surface.

♠

Very few women would feel comfortable married to a professional gambler. It takes a special kind of lady. She has to live with chance. The capital her gambler accumulates through the years is volatile, subject to be risked at any time for the sake of great gain. She waits for him to come home. Games go on all night. Games go on for days, weeks. He travels. She waits.

He says, "Honey, I'm down here in Amarillo, and it doesn't look like I'm going to make it home for a few more days. Guess I won't be able to take you to see Star Wars this week. Next week, I hope."

She's got to be able to simply say, "I miss you. How are we doing?" And then, depending on whether the news is good or bad, say either, "Oh, that's great!" or "Don't worry, baby, it will get better."

I need the security of having a family. A stable home, emotional support, love. There are hardly any women who can handle the sudden shifts in fortune that accompany the gambling life. It's too much of a burden to place on any woman. But there are a saintly few who can latch on to a gambling man and feel comfortable.

♠

Enter Shirley. At the country club, Bobby's father introduced him to a friend named Byron, a man in his late forties. Both skillful gin enthusiasts, he and Bobby spent many hours gambling at the game. For the most part Bobby won. A friendship developed, and Bobby began spending time at the Penthouse Club, a cocktail and dance establishment owned by the older man.

It was there that Bobby spotted Shirley.

"She seems really nice," he told Byron, nodding in the direction of Shirley, who was a cocktail waitress.

"She is really nice. Interested?"

"Just might be."

He began to visit the Penthouse Club even more regularly. Secretly his motive was to see Shirley. They talked casually and seemed to like each other. But there was no hint of romance. No love at first sight. Whenever he could collect a bit of information about Shirley, he'd add it to his mental catalog of data. He asked questions. Some of Shirley, but mostly he learned about her through quizzing Byron. Was she married? No, divorced and living with a boyfriend she'd been in love with for three years. What did she do in her spare time? She and the boyfriend went to night clubs sometimes. She was pretty much just a beautiful country girl who'd only begun to expand her horizons a few years ago. Well, could Byron arrange a *formal* introduction?

"You've met Bobby, haven't you, Shirley?" Byron said smoothly when the waitress neared the table where he and Bobby were sipping drinks.

"Sure have. We've talked some. That's your name . . . Bobby? Great, listen, I better get this drink over to Alex before he starts screaming." She smiled ever so warmly. Then she was gone.

Bobby grew even more intrigued by the young woman. He didn't consciously say to himself, "I want to have her," but that thought was pretty close to the surface of his brain. No so much that he was prepared to make an overt effort to gain her affection, but enough so he flirted with the idea.

The Penthouse Club had a pair of TVs, one at each end of the bar. Bobby always spent his Monday nights there watching the football game. Either he would sit toward the right end or the left end, depending on which seemed to be Shirley's station that evening. She'd ask how his team was doing and, unfortunately, he never had good news to give her. During this whole 1973 season, he hadn't won a single Monday night football game. And his Saturday and Sunday bets had also been a disaster. His bankroll needed attention. Somewhere he was going to have to find a way to pump it up.

They'd talk, he and Shirley. It got to the point where it was almost flirtation—quiet undertones that they didn't admit to each other, and not even to themselves. Bobby couldn't determine whether or not Shirley was taking an interest in him. But he kept hoping.

OBVIOUS TELL

Standing near the cigarette machine because there were no available seats, Byron and Bobby waded through fifteen minutes of small talk. Shirley brought their drinks. Instead of leaving immediately to tend to her duties on this crowded evening, she hung about holding a tray full of drinks.

Swaying subtly, sexily, she said, "I've just never seen it this busy."

And Bobby said, "Yeah, the band's all right!"

And she said, "I think they're really good."

"You getting good tips?" he asked.

"Uh-huh, pretty good."

Well, this went on for several minutes. It just seemed as if both of them lost track of time. Even in the noisy, chaotic environment that enveloped them, they felt hidden, alone and comfortable.

Finally Byron said, "Aren't there some people to be waited on." His voice was pleasant but firm.

"Oh, sorry!" said Shirley. She had forgotten, completely forgotten. Flustered and embarrassed, she wheeled to leave. But her eyes met Bobby's briefly and she tripped over his foot. She managed not to fall, managed to hang onto the tray. But all the drinks spilled. Everyone laughed, even Byron.

While Bobby helped Shirley gather the miraculously unbroken glasses, he felt certain that her insignificant chatter had not been altogether meaningless. *She's nervous,* he thought. *That means she's interested in me,* he reasoned.

♠

It was then that I formulated a game plan for winning Shirley. It was a long-range scheme, but I calmly and carefully pieced it together. Basically, it involved remaining gracious while never putting any pressure on her. She was so accustomed to guys making blatant and unwanted passes. I decided that if I acted directly opposite it might work. Besides, I had never been pushy by nature. Even during high school,

I'd never been able to ask a girl for a dance. I mean, I just froze solid. Anytime I wanted to dance, well, I'd just get a friend to lay the ground work. You know, get him to walk on over to where the girl was and drop subtle hints. Being too aggressive with women always made me feel nervous and uncomfortable.

Now, with my luck running bad and my bankroll depleted, I felt a powerful need for someone to share life with. Someone I could confide in, defining the pain I felt. Someone for sharing secrets. And, beyond any question whatsoever, I knew that person ought to be Shirley.

OPPORTUNITY

So it began. Shirley would wait on Bobby even if he wasn't seated in her station. On Monday nights, she'd take an interest in the televised football game.

"Which side, Bobby?"

"Well, I've got the blue guys, but they're not doing too swift."

Then she'd pull for Bobby's side, cheering whenever something went right, even though she knew nothing about football. But her vocal support didn't help. Bobby was into a streak where he was losing every game. It didn't matter what team he bet on, they just lost.

One night Shirley was less bubbly than usual. There was another waitress named Susan at the Penthouse Club—a good friend of Shirley's.

"I don't mean to be prying," Bobby spoke softly. "But is there something the matter with Shirley. I mean, maybe it's my imagination, but she doesn't seem quite herself."

"She had a fight with Richard."

"Much to it?"

"I think so. He left her at a bar. Just drove off and told her to find her own way home."

"Thanks, Susie, you're terrific."

Later, the first chance he got to talk to Shirley, Bobby said, "I hope you don't think I'm trying to be personal, but I hear you had a bad experience last night. Is there anything I can do? Anything that might be helpful?"

She said, no, there wasn't, but she opened up considerably and told Bobby the whole situation. "So Richard said he was leaving and stormed out. He's sort of hot tempered sometimes. I mean, this isn't the first time he's done it. He just gets mad at me sometimes and leaves me places. It's his way of punishing me."

Bobby considered his words carefully. *The game plan,* he reminded himself, *stick to the game plan.* "Well, if this ever happens again, Shirley, you've got a friend. You've got a way to get home."

Her waitress uniform consisted of hot pants, a jersey and boots. For over a month, Bobby never saw her in anything except that uniform. Then one night she came in unexpectedly to pick up her paycheck. She was more modestly attired, wearing brown slacks and a matching blouse. *Well, she just looks perfect,* Bobby thought. *She's gorgeous.* And if ever he had felt doubtful about the importance of maintaining his long-range game plan to win Shirley, he never questioned it thereafter.

She sat with him, and he said, "Could I buy you a drink?"

It ended up being many drinks, slowly sipped over polite, tentative conversation. Both felt that the talk was leading somewhere, but the destination remained undefined. Finally, he walked her to her car and said good night. He opened the door of her Pinto, but he didn't lean too close. He wanted to make her comfortable, uncrowded, wanted her to know she wasn't going to get nailed to the side of the Pinto. There was simply no threat of a good night kiss, and she knew it. That was part of the game plan. Bobby wanted to impress her with his manners.

Poker continued to keep his bankroll afloat, but he was melting away at football. Then even poker results went bad.

CHAPTER 16

High Stakes

STILLWATER, OKLAHOMA

He was on a two-session losing streak playing poker; football had been terrible and the previous night he'd played gin against a mere beginner and lost heavily.

It was a semi-private game held at the ranch house belonging to an oilman. A real, honest-to-God storybook Oklahoma oil millionaire. And a personable fellow, too. When Bobby had first been invited to this game, he'd felt honored. He'd been regularly attending another game in Stillwater, but this one was elite: This was the big leagues.

Never had a chance. Bobby just never had a chance.

The game was Hold 'em. Bobby had played it a few times, but he was up against players who'd lived with Hold 'em since they were teenagers. It's the game that's now used to determine the world champion. Each player holds a hand consisting of only two cards. The next cards are dealt face-up in the center of the table. First three at once, called the flop. Then the fourth card, then the fifth and final card. It's a variety of Seven-Stud where the players use the five face-up cards communally, in combination with the two cards they've been dealt, to make the best possible five-card poker hand.

The sophisticated twists and complications attached to Hold 'em had not yet sifted through the young Baldwin's mind. He still played at a low level of comprehension. His time wasn't yet.

In this game, besides the congenial, fifty-year-old host named Tyler, were two other bona fide millionaires, a couple of local ranchers and "Amarillo Slim" Preston. True, Slim *himself* was there—the tall slender Texan who had claimed the world title at Binion's Horseshoe Club in Vegas the previous year. Bobby had seen him interviewed on television just the previous night. It was the first time Bobby would compete against a top-rated professional.

Playing at this level of competition excited Bobby: He tried to impress Slim with his play. Twice he caught Tyler bluffing in big no-limit pots. He was electric with anticipation. By now he had $15,000 worth of chips in front of him, almost double his buy-in, and although he was playing bigger than his bankroll, he felt confident. He waited for the ultimate confrontation—with Slim and him tied into a big pot together. But it never happened.

About three and a half hours into the session, one of the ranchers moved all in for $20,000. Bobby held ace queen, and the flop had been king, queen, 6 of different suits. If the rancher held a king, Bobby knew it was all but over. And that's exactly what the man was representing by the size of the bet. A king-ace. Or even a pair of kings, queens or 6s, giving him three-of-a-kind. Possibly, he could even hold a pair of aces. Maybe, king-queen or king-6 or even queen-6. Those were the hands that could beat Bobby's ace-queen.

But there was a more insidious possibility. A bluff. The man had made only one substantial bet all night. That was a $12,000 wager, and Slim had folded. Bobby thought back, three times he could remember this rancher having a virtual lock on the pot, and each time the bet had been less than the size of the pot. Here was a pot with only $4,500 in it and the guy was betting $20,000. Could this be a bluff? Could the $12,000 he'd bet into Slim have been a bluff?

Bobby wondered aloud, "You got much?" He tried to keep his voice in control. He wanted to remain casual and make the other man do the worrying if, in fact, it was a bluff.

The opponent scarcely moved. Their eyes met and instinctively the man looked away. Then, he glared back at Bobby almost defiantly. Bobby reasoned this: If he really had the hand, he wouldn't have glanced away as soon as his eyes met mine. But he realized this mistake. He's intelligent and he knows that might have given his hand away. So he purposely looked right back into my eyes, pretending to be confident. But that's a cover-up. The man is bluffing. The man *is* bluffing! I know it!

Just to reinforce this conclusion, Bobby said, "It doesn't seem to me that you have anything." He watched the man very closely. He didn't seem to move. Frozen. A statue. And Bobby felt this was a good sign, because if this man really had the hand he was representing, he'd likely do something to encourage the call. Ten seconds passed, half a minute.

"I call what I have," Bobby said softly, sliding his stacks into the pot.

"That's a good call, son," said Amarillo Slim.

"Sure was," said the rancher shaking his head and turning over a 4 3. "Just thought I could get away with something. Didn't think you'd have the balls to call it, kid."

The next card was a 4, making a pair of 4s for the rancher. Then another 4, and suddenly Bobby's elation had evaporated. He had lost what he came with. His mind swirled with pain. *How can this happen to me? He's raking in all those chips, and they should have been mine . . .* But he said nothing. It wasn't his nature to get angry or to talk about his bad fortune. He just rose from the table, a little nervous but not showing it.

"That's enough for me. Thanks for the invitation. I enjoyed the game." And he left.

♠

It was sort of a graph down. Not a straight-line collapse. Ups and downs, but bigger downs. Football was just blowing me away. At the time it seemed almost supernatural. How could one man lose almost every game? I mean, sometimes I'd be winning until the last few seconds and then . . . well, it was plain hopeless.

Thinking back on that no-limit game in Stillwater, I realize that I made one very powerful mistake, even though that probably wasn't the reason I lost. The presence of Slim in the game had caused me to think mostly about what his reaction to my play would be, rather than letting my game play itself in a natural sort of way. You see this happen all the time when fairly decent players get in a game with big-name professionals. Their game just goes out the window.

Fancy. They try to be as fancy and creative as they can, thinking the name player will reach over and give them some kind of award or something. You almost always see them leave the table busted, tail between their legs, so to speak, feeling miserable because they played for the celebrity and not for themselves. And botched it up real good besides.

Pretty much, I'd made that same mistake. But driving home from the game, the cold hurt turned to warm anticipation. I just couldn't stop thinking about Shirley. It was during this dark drive home that I really got my head together and said, "Well, look, Bobby, you've got to be a little more forthright in your approach. Don't make her feel uneasy or fenced in, but make her know that you might be interested."

The next time I saw Shirley, she was talking about Corvettes. Seems a friend of hers had one and she'd ridden in it and was very impressed.

"Well, I've got a Corvette," I said. Extremely blasé, you know.

She said, surprised, "I thought you had a Thunderbird."

I'd walked her to her car several times by now, and in the lot she'd asked which my car was and I'd pointed out the blue T-Bird.

"Well, I have two cars," I said matter-of-factly. That was about all I had salvaged after the divorce. I almost never drove the Vette. Just didn't like it.

But now a bell went off in my head. She likes Corvettes!

"Who's the other one for?" Shirley wanted to know.

"Well, it's mine. I drive it almost all the time." A lie, but it seemed like the right strategy.

From then on, every trip I made to the Penthouse Club, I drove the Corvette. Certain things about me seemed to impress Shirley. My cars, gambling—my lifestyle. And I took advantage of that fact.

One weekend, Byron and I just took off for the Bahamas on the spur of the moment. I mean we were just sitting around talking and Shirley was listening. And Byron said, "Things are pretty slow. Let's go to Nassau for a couple of days."

I said, "Sure, why not." Just like that.

Well, this really impressed Shirley. When we got back, she was just full of questions to ask me. We got to feeling pretty close. Not that we were ready to confront each other, but the feeling was definitely there.

Then I got my chance.

JOSE'S CLUB

On Sunday's, the Penthouse Club was closed by Tulsa law, and many of its regular patrons gathered at a cocktail lounge outside the city limits. The place was called Jose's. Included in today's gathering were Bobby, Shirley and her boyfriend, Richard.

Something happened while Richard and Shirley danced. Bobby could see it transpiring—a hot flash of temper washing across the guy's face. Shirley looking angry, too. Harsh words. Bobby couldn't hear what was said because he was across the room and there was a live band.

Richard stormed out. Shirley was walking off the dance floor, a bit shaken. She was crying or *almost* crying, Bobby couldn't tell which. An inner longing told him to go over and comfort her. After all, Richard had left. But something made him hold back. It would seem too much like he'd been a vulture waiting. He had to take his time about it. Besides, Susan was there, and the two girls were now in a booth, engaged in a woman-to-woman talk. Bobby went to the bar and ordered a drink. While he waited, the girls came up behind him. It was about time for the club to close, nearly midnight.

Susan said, "I've got a date here . . ." She pointed to the man seated in a booth. "He's driving this Triumph two seater and, well—"

Shirley cut her off, still shaken by her spat with Richard, but suddenly finding the courage to speak for herself. "I could use a ride home, if it's not any trouble. I remember you said if I ev—"

"If you ever needed a way home, you had a friend," Bobby finished for her. "Shirley, you're more than welcome. I'll gladly take you wherever you want to go."

Looking at it from Bobby's point of view, you just couldn't have staged it any better. The fight, his happening to be there, the fact that it was almost closing time, Susan being on a date with a guy who was driving a two-seater.

They stopped for breakfast. When they left the coffee shop, it was two a.m. and she still didn't want to go home. She asked if he'd take her to an apartment she kept across town. It was a transitional hundred-dollar-a-month apartment she'd lived in after her divorce several years earlier. When she'd moved in with Richard, she kept the place because it was inexpensive and she had a lot of belongings there.

But when Bobby pulled up in front of the building, she looked like she were about to fall apart emotionally.

"Maybe you'd rather not do this," Bobby spoke quietly. He let his fingers soothe her hair, but not blatantly. He needed to offer comfort without it seeming like a pass. "You want me to take you to Richard's?" He felt fearful of an affirmative answer.

"No…"

They sat there for a long, long time and neither spoke. It became obvious she wasn't going to get out, that she didn't want to leave him.

He weighed his next words, wanting them to sound compassionate without any hint of being offensive. Finally, he said, "You know, you'd really be welcome to stay at my place. Until you feel better. You'd have a bedroom to yourself."

"Maybe . . ."

It was a very plush townhouse with expensive furnishings, and Bobby could tell she was instantly impressed. The first thing he did was cheat her at gin, just in a joking sort of way. It was a very clumsy effort. He'd simply look at the next card whenever he took one from the pack. When he confessed, she thought it was a wonderful and amazing feat.

More than a week passed, and there remained no physical relationship between them. Even so, a romance was blossoming. She took a keen interest in his gambling. For the first time in his life, he had someone to ease the pain when his luck ran bad. She listened, she cared. It was exactly what he needed while he watched his bankroll wither. And she reciprocated, telling him of her emotional troubles, of her daughter Staci who stayed mostly with a babysitter. She wanted to live with her daughter full-time.

Richard just played it slow. He felt Shirley still cared, and he was right. Possibly, sooner or later, she'd be back.

Bobby suffered at football. It seemed unreal, like a dark comedy.

CHAPTER 17

The Biggest Loss

SUNDAY, DECEMBER 16, 1973

He wagered roughly three-quarters of his bankroll, divided among five games. He bet both New York teams. With the Giants, he got two touchdowns, while he had to give two points with the Jets. He selected Atlanta and gave thirteen points, and he liked Chicago and six. Finally, he figured Denver could never beat a seven-and-a-half point spread against Oakland.

Nervously, he awaited his fate. The scores began to stack like doom upon doom. In the end it was:

Minnesota 31, New York Giants 7

Buffalo 34, New York Jets 14

Atlanta 14, New Orleans 10

Green Bay 21, Chicago 0

Oakland 21, Denver 17

He had lost them all.

He was so shaken that he couldn't talk to anyone right away, not even to Shirley. But just being beside her was a comfort. Her presence partially soothed the agony in his soul. He had lived through a fantasy win in Las Vegas, lost it all, rebuilt, lost it all, rebuilt, lost it all. And each time he'd resolved to hang on to the next bankroll. But again, it was gone. The pain this time, following weeks of battering by the football bookmakers, was scarcely tolerable. At least there was Shirley.

CONFRONTATION

They entered an after hours club, seated themselves at a booth and ordered drinks.

"Richard's here." Bobby tried to sound nonplussed, but the presence of Shirley's former lover rattled him. He wanted her to feel comfortable. Especially tonight.

"I know." But she obviously didn't feel as casual as her pretense. No, there were strong signs that she still cared about Richard and that, perhaps, she remained deeply in love with him.

Then it happened. Richard waved Shirley over to his table. She smiled nervously, first at Richard, then at Bobby and said, almost inaudibly, "I better go talk to him."

She left her drink. They stood, Richard and Shirley, far across the room and talked. Together, they seemed so much like a pair that, after a few minutes, Bobby couldn't watch. He just stared at his drink, sipped it and waited. It was apparent to Bobby that Richard was asking her to come back. And she seemed to be standing closer to him now than when they'd begun talking. Obviously she was undecided, but Bobby's mind for some reason kept spilling out football scores. Bad beat after bad beat these past weeks—Los Angeles 26, Chicago 0; San Francisco 38, Philadelphia 28; Baltimore 16, Miami 3—and he felt that it was just fate that had grabbed him, pinned him in the mud and refused to let go.

Thinking about Shirley, the hurt was too much. Fifteen minutes passed. Twenty minutes. He tried to be philosophical. He'd stuck to his game plan. He'd played the hand the best way he knew how, and all that remained was for the players to turn their cards over and see who took the pot.

That's how he tried to look at it. But an overwhelming sense of destiny numbed him. St. Louis 32, Atlanta 10; Detroit 40, Chicago 7. He just couldn't win a game.

♠

I kept telling myself that I wasn't going to break. No matter what the gods of fortune spilled on me, I would survive. That's what I told myself, but the agony grew inside me with every minute that Shirley stayed away. Finally she walked toward me. Richard ambled in the other direction, kind of smug, I thought.

Shirley sat down at the booth across from me. Probably a half hour had passed, but it seemed like a week or a month. My suspicion was that she was going to let me down easy. I mean, I could just feel it, and I thought, well, that's the way it's going to be, I'm just not supposed to win anything. There wasn't any spirit left in me, no fight left, I was sapped. I couldn't even make my eyes meet hers.

Finally, I said, "Would you like a fresh drink?" Still, I didn't look at her directly.

"No." That made me think that maybe she was just going to break me the bad news softly and leave.

But the silence between us just went on and on while the band seemed oblivious to my agony. Rock n' Roll. Gradually, Shirley began to drum her fingers to the beat.

At last I got the nerve to ask, "Do you want to tell me anything about it?"

She said, sort of remotely, "Richard apologized. He wants me back . . ." So on and so forth.

You know, she never told me what she'd decided. But pretty soon I got to thinking, Well, hell, Bobby. She's still sitting here, and Richard, he's across the room somewhere. I put it together. I didn't ask her any more questions. We left the club together.

And when we got home, I said, "You know, I'd like to have Staci move in. She'd be like my own daughter, if that's what you want . . ."

So Staci came to live with us the next day.

♠

Over the next several weeks, he managed to lift his meager bankroll up to almost respectable proportions playing poker. The games were soft, and his attitude was right. Shirley made the difference. But his gains at poker were diluted by gin rummy losses. He had befriended a man named Frank. In spite of the losses Bobby suffered playing gin against the less-skilled middle-aged man, their friendship flourished. In scarcely a month, Frank had become almost a second father to Bobby. Meanwhile, football continued to batter Bobby's bankroll. On the afternoon that he went to Frank's hotel room, he had only $3,600.

"Beer?"

"No thanks, Frank. I just don't ever drink and play."

Frank opened himself a can nonetheless. They played for $400 a game. Bobby lost ten out of the first twelve decisions, putting him $3,200 in the hole.

Each man placed $400 beneath an ashtray—the stake for the next game. This would have to be Bobby's last game, if he lost.

On the first hand, he thought he spotted something . . . something he couldn't believe . . . something he didn't *want* to believe. It seemed that possibly a card had disappeared from the top of the deck and gone into Frank's palm. It must have been a mistake. But just to make sure, Bobby quietly counted the remaining cards after Frank ginned.

One short!

Bobby felt hurt and betrayed, but he waited. On the next hand, summoning his courage, he reached across the table and grabbed Frank's wrist. The 3 of spades popped out of the man's hand.

"I think you've got an extra card there." That was all Bobby said. Neither man spoke, there was nothing to say. Quietly, stunned, Bobby took the $800 from under the ash tray and left the hotel. Frank, $2800 richer than when they'd sat down to play, did nothing to prevent Bobby from leaving.

Jesus, thought Bobby, walking briskly to his car, *he's been cheating me all along.* When he reached his apartment, all sorts of things raced through his mind. What should he do? He'd been cheated out of most of his precious remaining bankroll. Should he get a gun? Should he demand his money back? Perhaps, he should go to the man's wife and expose the bastard . . . But, no, he decided to let it slide. Next time he'd be a little smarter. Having so decided, Bobby kicked at a newspaper near the entrance to his apartment. It was a rare show of temper. Out of character.

But finally, he'd been driven to it. Too many bad beats linked together. The docile, controlled Baldwin had finally lost his cool for a moment. Even this, though, went badly. He missed the paper, hit the concrete step and fractured his toe.

"Ow! Damn it!" he screamed hopping about painfully. "Damn it! Damn it!"

♠

You just can't imagine how bad things got. Continuing to bump my head against the goal posts, so to speak, I managed to lose every playoff game. Then I bet Minnesota to win the Super Bowl. Miami took it 24-7.

Still, there was Shirley to keep my spirits from washing beneath the tide. By late February, things had become so dismal that all we had left, all the money we had in the world, was about thirty dollars on the dresser. A good deal of that was in change, quarters, dimes, nickels and, yes, pennies.

Pennies! For the first time I could ever remember, those dull and ugly one-centers had at least a modicum of value. Pretty soon we had spent all the bills, and the quarters were disappearing. And I remember spending the last silver coins on gasoline. God, I felt pretty ridiculous handing four dollar's worth of small change to the service station attendant. It was time for me and Shirley to have a serious talk.

♠

Shirley said, "Sometimes it looks really dark and then, all of a sudden, things get better. Lots better." They sat together on the couch, and she stroked his forearm lovingly. This was her warrior, this Bobby, and she believed in him.

After a while, he said, "God, I just can't believe Frank would do that to me. It just seems so . . . I don't know, I just can't understand . . ."

"People aren't usually the way you want them to be. That's what you told me once. You haven't mentioned anything about Frank for a week. I thought you were getting over it."

"Do you know how much money we have, total?"

"I know it's not very much, Bobby, but—"

"One hundred and sixty-six pennies! I just counted them. There's not even a dime or nickel left. Just pennies."

"Well, we can probably borrow some."

"No! I've got to think about you and Staci, about being honorable. I owe $70,000 in football bets. Nobody's giving me any pressure, but . . ."

"But the pressure comes from in here," she finished for him, placing a hand on his chest.

He smiled. She understood. As always, she understood.

"You'll be able to pay it back. Maybe it will take a little time, but I know you can do it."

"A man, George, up in Oklahoma City offered me a job. It's just $40 a night dealing craps at the club he runs. But I think I ought to take it."

"If you think it's the right thing, then that's what you should do."

"I'm going to drive up there tomorrow, and I'll send for you and Staci as soon as I can. I'll call you every night."

"You going to see your parents before you go?"

"No. Shirley, I can't talk to them, not right now, not like this. Maybe you could give them a call for me and . . ."

"I'll take care of it."

He arrived in Oklahoma City with six cents, having gone to the bank, exchanged his previous pennies for a dollar bill, two quarters, and a dime, then promptly spent that on gasoline. He'd had somewhere between a quarter and a half tank, and he figured that this extra $1.60 worth would just about put him at his destination. He figured correctly. When he reached the parking lot of the private club where he'd been hired, the car was sputtering, and he actually coasted to a stop. Empty!

He was totally inexperienced at handling a craps game, but the older, patient George showed him what to do.

"You'll do just fine, Bobby. That's the reason I asked you to help out. You can handle anything . . ."

He slept the first two nights in his car without letting anyone know about it. He'd just quietly slip into the back seat and cover himself with a jacket. Once he heard voices outside. Seemed like high school age boys. One said, "Hey, there's someone in this car."

"Yeah, probably a drunk."

"Maybe it's some guy blew his paycheck in George's club and he don't want to go home and face his old lady."

"Yeah, maybe . . ." And the youths walked away, their voices getting fainter. Only then did Baldwin open his eyes. He had pretended to remain asleep, not wanting to face anyone at this low point in his life, not even strangers.

The club catered to a high-class clientele including doctors, lawyers, businessmen and local gamblers. The games played were craps, blackjack, and Hold 'em poker. A longtime friend of Bobby's named Terry was also helping George run the show. It was on the third night that Terry discovered Bobby in the car.

He tapped on the rear window. A somewhat embarrassed Bobby, said, "Hi, Terry, how you doing?"

"You're not sleeping *here!* It's cold out."

"Well, you know, this seemed like it was real close and convenient. I just haven't had time to find a place yet."

"Uh-huh. Until you do get the time to find a place, Bobby, I'd like you to stay with me. There's plenty of room."

Two days later, at Terry's generous insistence, Bobby phoned Shirley. He told her to grab what she could and move to Oklahoma City. She and Staci arrived two days thereafter.

Still, it wasn't a proud time for Bobby. They found a regular sitter for Staci, and Shirley took a job. Bobby tried to gather a bankroll. Terry was into baseball, spending a lot of time keeping statistics and planning his bets. Bobby took a piece of this action but, like it had been with football, he seldom won a bet.

He sat down with Shirley, finally, and talked about his ambitions as a professional gambler. It seemed obvious that he should give up betting sports. So he resolved to quit.

As soon as they had $1,000 saved, they moved into their own apartment. It cost $200 a month, and it made them happy.

Bobby and Terry pooled their money and formed an informal partnership. Whenever either man played gin, poker, blackjack, pool, anything, the other had half the action. There was one exception.

"Anytime you get to wanting to bet football, baseball, basketball or anything like that, Terry, deal me out." Bobby had made a firm promise to himself to drop sports betting. And he would honor that promise forever.

Their bankroll grew, and Bobby did more than his share to make it happen.

CHAPTER 18

Hold 'Em

I didn't especially like dealing craps. George shifted me over to blackjack, but I didn't truly enjoy the job until he transferred me to the poker table. The game was Hold 'em. I learned more dealing than I had in years of actual playing. I really focused on the game, and not just on the cards. I concentrated on the players. And I was getting pretty proficient at reading people. My ability at Hold 'em probably tripled while I was dealing the game. Without playing a hand, I grew from fairly good to nearly top level.

Naturally, I was eager to test these skills.

COMMON MISTAKES

MISTAKE ONE:
Slow playing big pairs before the flop

There's just no surer way to get broke.

MISTAKE TWO:
Playing an ace with a small suited card too strongly

This is one of the costliest errors a novice can make. Ace-4 suited simply isn't much of a Hold 'em hand.

MISTAKE THREE:
Staying for the flop with hands like K 3 and Q 6

Unpaired starting hands where you can't flop a straight or a flush should never be played. That *includes* hands with an ace.

MISTAKE FOUR:
Playing weak hands from the front

The more players that remain to act behind you, the stronger your hand must be. This is much more vital in Hold 'em than in Seven-Stud because when you act first in Hold 'em, you act first on every round of betting through the entire hand.

MISTAKE FIVE:
Drawing to the ignorant end

In Hold 'em it is so unwise to go for the low side of a straight that the practice has become known as drawing at the "ignorant end." For example: If the flop is 8 7 6, you want to be holding a 9 and not a 5.

MISTAKE SIX:
Attempting to bluff when the flop includes a jack and a 10

When the flop comes J 10 4, many unsophisticated players figure there's a good opportunity to buy one. That's absolutely false. There's virtually no rational hand your opponent could be playing that wouldn't provide him with a pair, two pair, trips or a straight draw.

MISTAKE SEVEN:
Betting aggressively into uniform flops

Any three cards in sequence constitute a uniform flop. When you hold two kings and 8 9 10 flops, beware!

MISTAKE EIGHT:
Getting tied to a big pair

Whenever you begin with two queens in the pocket and the flop is 9 6 2, you have a trouble hand if anyone bets, especially in no-limit games. Many opponents are unlikely to play small cards, and if they do, they're not likely to bet just one pair. You're very often facing a bigger pair, a straight or flush draw, two pair, or three of a kind.

You might have the best hand and you might win, but you've got a problem.

FINAL FORMULA

RULE ONE:

Don't slow play big pairs before the flop.

RULE TWO:

Play an ace with a small suited card cautiously, if at all.

RULE THREE:

Play only strong hands from early positions.

RULE FOUR:

Don't draw to the ignorant end.

RULE FIVE:

Consider folding a big pair when you get action following a small flop.

RULE SIX:

When you begin with a big pair, put the action in *before* the flop. Thereafter play cautiously unless you improve.

RULE SEVEN:

Ordinarily, do most of your gambling immediately after the flop.

RULE EIGHT:

Play two-way draws aggressively. (That includes hands with both a straight and a flush possible and hands with a pair plus a potential straight or flush.)

RULE NINE:

If you're trying for an open-end straight-flush, play very aggressively.

RULE TEN:

When you hold a big pair against a uniform flop, play cautiously.

RULE ELEVEN:

Never try to bluff into a flop that includes a jack and a 10.

RULE TWELVE:

Never play an unsuited hand that includes both ends of a straight.

RULE THIRTEEN:

Any two non-connecting cards (cards that leave no straight possible on the flop) are usually unplayable.

CHAPTER 19

On the Road

LUBBOCK, TEXAS

"Take the pot!" barked a middle-aged Texan, losing his cool momentarily and shoving the chips angrily in Bobby's direction. "If you can find a way to call a sixteen thousand dollar bet on a pair of 6s when there's hardly two grand out there . . . well . . . well . . . well, just take the pot!"

The man regained his composure, straightened his western jacket and left the table, saying, "See you boys next week."

An hour later, a conservatively dressed accountant shook his head miserably and said, "Good bet, Bobby. I sure thought you were trying to buy it. Well, that's me for tonight." He, too, left.

Within twenty minutes, Bobby had personally busted two more players. It was then that the host, a burly man in his mid-thirties, said calmly, "Unless anyone wants to play four-handed, I'll just cash you out early."

It was one of those rare games on the circuit where all transactions are handled in money instead of on paper. The other two remaining men cashed out and left. Then the host counted Bobby's chips and gave him $38,000 in hundred dollar bills.

"That's quite a score, Bobby. I'm genuinely impressed with your game, son, genuinely impressed. But sometimes it pays to hold back a little, take it easy. You're welcome to come again next week, but try to keep that in mind."

♠

I hadn't learned certain realities about private games. First, you always give consideration to the host. You've been honored with an invitation, and as an invited guest, you've got to keep his interests in mind. Likely as not, he's spent years culturing and fine-tuning his game. He has invited you because you have a reputation for manners and fair play. He doesn't mind you winning, or even winning big. But if you break-up the game, then he's in a spot where he has to worry about whether all his people will be back again next time. So, second, never be the cause of a private game breaking up early.

Usually there are three or four consistent winners in these private gatherings. For the most part, these are not professional gamblers, but just players who have developed superior skills. Also, the typical game has one, sometimes two, producers. A producer is a pleasure player who generally has a lot of money and whose involvement in poker is so casual that he seldom, if ever, wins. The producer is an important person to the non-pro winners that frequent every game. And he's the most important asset the host has.

A third rule to remember is: Never go out of your way to break the producer. The regular players will consider it an unkind gesture. Many times, after the game has disbanded, the heavy loser, the producer, has tried to get me into head-up action. Almost always, I turn him down, trying to seem as gracious as possible. I might say, "Well, I'm really very tired." Or, "I've got to be back in Tulsa by morning." The man who runs the game and all the regular players appreciate this action. You make yourself welcome. This far-sighted strategy means more money for you in the long run, even though you must sacrifice some easy scores now and then.

GEORGE'S CLUB
MARCH, 1974

Although, Bobby traveled every chance he got, he still dealt the poker game in Oklahoma City four nights a week. George had cut him in for twenty percent of the poker action. That profit was earned by raking small amounts from the pots, never more than five percent.

By now Bobby had managed to pay off most of what he owed to the bookmaker in Tulsa. His *real* bankroll was almost positive again.

There was an Oklahoma City bookie named Brady—a tall slender man nearing sixty who spat tobacco. The man had an annoying habit of always coughing in faces, and he usually had nothing pleasant to say. He was the sort of fellow who'd complain about anything, even when fate had been kind. Nobody liked him. Even Bobby, who seldom felt unkindly toward any human being, confided to his easygoing friend Terry that Brady was beginning to get on his nerves.

"He's got a lot of bread," Terry pointed out.

"True."

"And he plays pool. Not as good as you do, Bobby, but he plays. Interested?"

"Sure."

"I'll see what can be arranged."

"How's our bankroll?" Bobby asked. "I mean, would you have any objections to my playing Brady no limit head-to-head?"

"That sounds all right, too. What game does he want to play."

"Deuce-to-Seven. I've played it a few times."

"Well, go to it, Bobby. Let's give it a shot."

Brady was obnoxious, making far more than his share of hands and, instead of simply raking in the pots graciously, he badgered Bobby. He'd say, "Tough luck, kid, but I'm glad it's you and not me." He'd gloat, "You're playing with an all-star, kid. Shove me that pot, baby!" He'd snicker every time he went in with the worst hand and drew out on Bobby.

On the last hand, Bobby drew one card to 9 6 4 2 and caught a queen. Brady drew two and made a 6. Nothing to it. Bobby and Terry had just blown the biggest part of their combined bankroll.

"You just can't go up against the big boys and expect to win," Brady leered, stacking the chips.

Just then there was a thud at the main door. The building trembled, and the wooden bolt across the door creaked in agony. Again. The same sound. Bobby's heart raced. His mind was awash with photo-like remembrances of the kidnapping attempt at the Bridge Club. He'd also been involved in a hijacking a month earlier where two men had muscled their way into a game in Denver and taken all the cash. Bobby had lost only $600 that time, having arranged credit in advance with the man who ran the game. But what he did remember, the really frightening thing, was that those men had barged in with *machine guns!* Machine guns right in the midst of civilized America.

A cracking noise now at the front door. The beam failed to hold and splintered into two pieces. Men charged in.

This time it wasn't highjackers. This time it was the police. Here it was April, and it was a cold, cold night. Freezing temperature. A blast of the cold air swept across the room immediately.

"Nobody move!"

It was something Bobby had been expecting. The cops were getting tough on private gambling in Oklahoma. It was a new all-out campaign against outlaws. In the somewhat provincial mentality of Oklahoma police, poker players were outlaws.

"Everyone on the floor!" yelled the meanest cop of them all. So everyone got on the floor. The cops left the door open and kept customers and employees alike on the floor for nearly an hour while they smashed the dice, blackjack and poker tables.

Terry and Bobby lay shivering side by side, fearful of movement, because the cops seemed to be in a particularly hostile mood, barking, "Keep still!" and "I *said* face down!" whenever they spotted the slightest infraction of their orders.

"These guys aren't too happy," Terry tried to joke.

"I think they're downright rude," said Bobby.

Locked in the cell, waiting to be released, Bobby and Terry got a good chance to talk to Brady, the bookie. The conversation got steered around to pool, and a match was scheduled. It would take place immediately upon their release at Brady's house.

It was just past two in the morning when the bookie admitted them to his home. Terry sat anxiously on a love seat and watched. It was a magnificent pool table, and the bookie showed considerable skill. But he was outclassed. Bobby took their meager bankroll, devastated by this same opponent earlier that evening, and ran it into more than $50,000.

"I quit," said Brady. "What about you, Terry. Wanna shoot some pool?" His annoying tone didn't pack its usual sting.

"Sure," said Terry.

But Bobby pulled his good friend aside and said, "Terry, if you play this man, I don't want any part of it." Terry was stunned by that.

"I can beat him."

"Terry," Bobby repeated firmly. "I don't want any part of it."

Terry played anyway, and lost the half of the bankroll that rightfully belonged to him. Bobby and Terry would maintain their informal partnership off and on for the next two years. But for the time being, they were no longer a team.

Bobby paid off the last of his debt to the Tulsa bookmaker. The nightmare of being financially buried had ended. Now there was new light. No debts, and a starting bankroll of $19,000. He hit the road.

TRINIDAD, COLORADO

He dialed his home number.

"Honey, I'm sorry I couldn't phone you sooner. The game just went on and on."

"How'd you do?"

"Good. Won about thirty thousand. There's a game I've been invited to tomorrow night. I'll try to make it home in two days. Miss you."

"I miss you, too."

PLAINVIEW, TEXAS

"I'll be driving home tomorrow. Tell Staci I'm bringing a present."

"Sounds like it went all right."

"These games are really soft. I picked up another twenty-four thousand tonight."

"Bobby, that's wonderful."

"Things won't always go this well, Shirley. But it feels nice."

"Hurry home."

SHREVEPORT, LOUISIANA

For a year things had gone successfully. His expertise at cards had reached a level where he could sit in virtually any poker game as a big favorite. He also registered a profit playing gin. Bridge had become an important game to him and suddenly, within a year, he rose from a novice to Life Master.

Wherever he went now, any time he sat in a game, his reputation as a skilled player preceded him. Among the pro circuit in Oklahoma, Colorado, Texas, Louisiana, and Arkansas, he was admired. He began to make regular appearances at big-league games, and began to socialize on an egalitarian level with the big names in poker:

Doyle Brunson, Johnny Moss, Puggy Pearson, Sailor Roberts, Amarillo Slim.

Bobby Baldwin had almost arrived.

His bankroll was approaching $200,000. In fact, it had gone past that on one occasion, only to drop to $135,000 the following night. Sure, there were fluctuations, but the trend seemed clear. He was building a permanent bankroll.

A MAJOR OPPORTUNITY

"What's his name?" Bobby asked.

"Edwards. Tom Edwards," Puggy Pearson said. "He told me to pass along the invitation. He's just one of those poker nuts. You know, wants to bump up against the best players he can find. You and me are invited, plus four other Louisiana locals he considers real strong. Thing is, they're *not* strong, so it looks like easy pickin's to me."

"Well, Puggy, the way you're saying this, it sounds like a big game. Just how big is it going to *be?*"

"First off, Edwards wanted to just play someone heads-up for half a million dollars. His game is Deuce to Seven. I told him I might be interested. Then he said, how 'bout a ring game. Get seven guys together and they all put up half a million. So I told him, look, you're never going to find seven guys willing to put three and a half million on the table. It just isn't reasonable."

"How big is this going to *be?*" Baldwin asked again, astounded by the magnitude of this invitation.

"You can buy in for a hundred and fifty thou."

Bobby shook his head negatively. "You'll have to deal me out on this one, Puggy." His bankroll just wasn't big enough.

It would be reckless.

It was out of the question.

"How good is this Edwards?" Bobby demanded.

♠

Edwards wasn't very good at all. Neither were the others he'd invited. It was the biggest game I'd ever played in—over a million dollars on the table. And the only talent in the game was me and Puggy. He did all right, but me, I just faded away from the very beginning. The gods of Deuce-to-Seven Lowball were in a vindictive mood, I guess. During the six hours I played, I made only a couple minor mistakes.

Even though my game wasn't in top form that night, it was clear that both Puggy and I were monster favorites: Well, it was clear to me, anyway. Not clear, though, to Tom Edwards who kept raking in one pot after another.

The buy-in was $150,000 per man. That's what I lost, too. All of it. Then I drove home to Shirley, not even bothering to stop at a motel, because I would have been unable to sleep anyway.

When I unlocked the door to my apartment, it was seven in the morning. Both Staci and Shirley still slept. The first thing I did was take a quick audit. When all the assets and debits were weighed, I scribbled this figure on a note pad: $38,331. That was what I had left.

By then Shirley was awake and came sleepily from the bedroom to wrap her arms about me.

"How'd it go?"

"Poorly." I didn't elaborate.

Deuce-to-Seven is primarily a Southern game, usually played no-limit. Other than Hold 'em, Deuce-to-Seven has been my biggest moneymaker, but in Shreveport, the poker gods had been sadistic.

Discards:

Cards held: 4♣ 2♦ 7♣

Deuce-to-Seven: Any two-card draw must include a deuce.

CHAPTER 20

Deuce-to-Seven Low

COMMON MISTAKES

MISTAKE ONE:

Playing loose from an early position.

Deuce-to-Seven is a close relative of Ace-to-Five Lowball. Deuce-to-Seven, however, is traditionally a no-limit game, and getting out of line in an early position, when there are many opponents waiting to act afterward, can be vastly more dangerous.

MISTAKE TWO:

Building large pots with medium hands.

Try for small pots with medium-strength hands. Try for big pots with quality hands. Obvious, right? Well, I suspect that most players fail to keep that in mind in no-limit Deuce-to-Seven. Otherwise why would they habitually trap themselves with second-best hands, like rough 9s, in monstrous pots? Otherwise why would they be content to take tiny pots with 7s? Silly as it may seem, keep reminding yourself when you have a hand of moderate strength, "I want to win this without committing myself to a large pot." And when you have the nuts, tell yourself, "I won't be content to win just a token amount."

MISTAKE THREE:

Not giving sufficient respect to an early-position raiser.

Caution is mandatory when an opponent brings it in from an early seat. He's risking more, because there are more opponents left that can pounce on him. So, usually, he'll have a stronger hand than he would in a later position. And you need to take that into consideration when deciding to compete for the pot.

MISTAKE FOUR:
Drawing at open-end straights.

In Deuce-to-Seven where, unlike ace-to-five, straights and flushes count against you, this can be a disastrous policy.

MISTAKE FIVE:
Making two-card draws that exclude a deuce.

All quality two-card tries should include a deuce.

MISTAKE SIX:
Standing pat between two players when you hold a vulnerable hand.

This is a very common error in all no-limit games, particularly Deuce-to-Seven.

FINAL FORMULA

RULE ONE:

Play tight from early positions; play loose from late positions.

RULE TWO:

Keep in mind that you want to be involved in *small* pots with medium-strength hands and *large* pots with quality hands.

RULE THREE:

Always respect an opponent who raises the blind from an early position.

RULE FOUR:

Seldom draw to open-end straights and *never* from an early position.

RULE FIVE:

Any two-card draw must include a deuce.

RULE SIX:

Never stand pat between two players unless you intend to call.

RULE SEVEN:

Any quality one-card draw must include a deuce or a 3.

CHAPTER 21

Your Bankroll

My efforts to reestablish a bankroll failed. I just couldn't put it together. Poker was a spinning-the-wheels endeavor. Win some, lose some. Gin was a disaster. Since the police were really getting tough with poker games in Oklahoma, we moved to Dallas.

The games there were soft. My bankroll fluctuated between $10,000 and $50,000 for a few months. Then winter came, the winter of 1975, and it was a bad period for me. My luck was just rotten, and I didn't have the good sense to step down. I was still bashing my skull into the bricks, trying to play games for which my bankroll was inadequate. Almost overnight, I found myself nearly broke.

Shirley tried to soothe my agonies. Stable Shirley, understanding Shirley, optimistic Shirley. Truly a gambler's woman.

Everything was terrible. We got a little behind on the bills. The rent was due. It was a cold winter for Dallas. And I was in this game, a smaller game because I couldn't afford the games I'd grown accustomed to, and I was winning good. I was up two or three thousand, and it was only a $20-limit game. So I was in very good shape.

Shirley phoned me at the club.

"The landlord came by and he doesn't seem too patient. What should I tell him about the rent."

"Tell him I'll pay it in the morning."

"Are we doing good?"

"Pretty fair, Shirley. I've got a couple of thousand here in front of me. Go to sleep and don't worry about the bills. Looks like we won't have to do without electricity after all."

She laughed. She seemed so happy, so relieved.

But then things just got awful. I didn't have the sense to quit. Just watched my winnings wash away. Finally, I was down to a three hundred dollar profit, enough to take care of the bills, but not enough to play again tomorrow.

So I said to myself, you've got to have a bankroll. I continued to play. Lost the three hundred profit, and pretty soon lost the two hundred I'd come with.

I felt miserable when I got home. Shirley woke up and said, "Everything okay?"

Well, I just wanted her to go back to sleep. I didn't want her to share the pain with me right then. So I said, "Everything's fine, sugar." She seemed so content. She just rolled over and started dreaming.

The next morning I had to tell her the truth.

She's so strong, you know, so very strong. The only thing she said was, "We'll figure out something."

We scraped together a little money. A week later I went into a small private game with $50 and doubled it. Things got good in a hurry.

By springtime, I had a bankroll approaching $100,000. And I got to thinking, Bobby, you're doing something wrong. You keep building these bankrolls, one right after another, and they just seem to vanish. You're definitely doing something wrong! I really gave it a lot of thought.

COMMON MISTAKES

MISTAKE ONE:
Playing bigger than your bankroll

No matter how good you are, if you continually tackle games you can't afford, sooner or later you'll string two or three losses together and get broke. Remember, you won't be a successful gambler unless you can stay in action.

MISTAKE TWO:
Reluctance to limit losses

Unless you decide in advance how much you can prudently lose, you're apt to find it difficult to back off under stress.

MISTAKE THREE:
Refusal to step down in class

If things are going poorly and your bankroll is in jeopardy, try a smaller game for a few sessions.

MISTAKE FOUR:
Letting your ego take over

Sure, if you take pride in your poker ability, it's hard to back away from challenges. But sometimes you're hopelessly outclassed because you don't know the other man's game very well. Ego also chews up many bankrolls because players like to get even with opponents who bluff them. Play your cards. In the long run, your ego *will* be pacified by your success.

MISTAKE FIVE:
Treating poker as entertainment

It's all right to *enjoy* playing poker. But if you also *respect* it, play very *seriously*.

MISTAKE SIX:
Playing under emotional stress

When you have personal problems, you're apt to be unable to make critical decisions. Sometimes it's better to stay home until you come to grips with your psyche.

MISTAKE SEVEN:
Absence of a game plan

If you don't have a long term strategy carefully laid out, it's easy to play fast and loose with your bankroll.

MISTAKE EIGHT:
Playing soft

When you start making friendly gestures at the poker table—like not raising because you feel sorry for an opponent—it's difficult to play with the intensity required to maintain a bankroll.

MISTAKE NINE:
Unwillingness to seek advice

This is an ego problem. Your game may drift off course. It happens to all professionals from time to time. Don't feel too proud to ask someone you respect to evaluate your game.

MISTAKE TEN:
Bad manners

You can't build a bankroll if people won't play against you.

MISTAKE ELEVEN:
Carrying large sums of money

The most abrupt way to lose a bankroll is to get robbed. When you earn a reputation for honesty and can play on credit, you'll be able to attend private games without jeopardizing your bankroll and your life by walking around with a thick wad of hundred-dollar bills.

MISTAKE TWELVE:
Deviating too frequently from your best game

Yes, I've stressed that you've got to mix it up and play the other man's game from time to time. But the healthiest thing you can do for your bankroll is to stick with whatever game you're best at playing.

FINAL FORMULA

RULE ONE:

Never risk more than 15% of your bankroll at a single session.

RULE TWO:

Set a limit on your losses *in advance*.

RULE THREE:

Be willing to play smaller games temporarily when your bankroll warrants such action.

RULE FOUR:

Don't let your ego play your cards.

RULE FIVE:

Treat poker as a business, never as entertainment.

RULE SIX:

Know your opponents, and don't play if you're even slightly suspicious of the game.

RULE SEVEN:

Don't play under emotional stress.

RULE EIGHT:

Have a long-range game plan.

RULE NINE:

Always play hard.

RULE TEN:

Occasionally ask other strong players for advice.

RULE ELEVEN:

Conduct yourself as a gentleman.

RULE TWELVE:

Carry as little cash as possible.

RULE THIRTEEN:

Play primarily your best game.

RULE FOURTEEN:

Develop a reputation for honesty.

*(above) Bobby and son, B.J. (below) Bobby's daughter Staci, with family.
"I need the security of having a family. A stable home, emotional support,
love. " – B.B.*

Bobby and wife, Donna

CHAPTER 22

Emergence of a Superstar

I just wasn't quite ready. Not enough experience in tournaments. Before the first day of competition, I had lunch with Doyle Brunson who, although he had never won this tournament, was considered by most to be the best no-limit player in the world.

"How you think I'll do?" I asked him.

"You'll do okay," Brunson said softly. Then, as if inspired, he said, "How 'bout a friendly wager. Two thousand says I'll last longer than you will."

Worst bet I ever made. Doyle won the tournament.

Next year, Doyle greeted me as soon as I set foot in the Horseshoe Club. "Are we on?" he asked.

"On?"

He smiled broadly and, in his typically gentle manner, said, "Sure, for two thousand. We could make the same bet as last year."

"No, way!" I teased. "You'd have to spot me something."

"All right. I'll give you two-to-one."

Second worst bet I ever made. Doyle won the championship again!

The next year, I said, "Don't even ask, Doyle. I'm not betting you this year, so you'll just have to scrape up two grand somewhere else."

Worst laydown I ever made. I won the title!

As soon as Bobby took steps to keep his bankroll from being perpetually threatened, his career blossomed. Poker was now such a scientific enterprise for him that he spent long nights *away* from the poker table going over hands and planning even more devastating strategies for the next game.

He began a long tour as a traveling player, taking a few days off every week to fly back to Dallas to be with Shirley and Staci. His first stop on the April Texas tour was Waco. There he won $11,000. Then more wins: $22,000 in Austin; $3,500 in San Antonio; $42,000 in Corpus Christi; a small loss of $1100 in Kerrville; wins of $39,000 in San Angelo, $18,000 in Sweetwater and $84,000 in Amarillo. And never during this swing did he place his bankroll in jeopardy.

In May, 1976 he decided to tackle the best in the world at the championship Hold 'em event. There were twenty-three entrants, putting up a stake of $10,000 each. Bobby made the final table, finishing eighth. Considering the competition, he wasn't dissatisfied with this effort.

Between his first participation in the Horseshoe Club's *World Series of Poker* and his return the second time, there was a year of tedious effort. He had never taken poker so seriously.

When he didn't know something, he asked. His phone bill was enormous. Whenever he needed a solution to a poker problem, he'd dial up Doyle Brunson or Amarillo Slim and get an opinion. When he needed a mathematical answer, he'd phone a mathematician. When he wanted insight into a psychological matter, he'd call a noted psychologist. He devised methods to read players that put his game far above the level of the average professional.

Still, he polished his game. Returning to Binion's Horseshoe Club in May of 1977, he felt ready. Poker had become an obsession, and the days of treating it frivolously were long, long dead.

He entered the Seven-Stud world championship against eight other pros and won it. It was only a $45,000 first prize, but it gave Bobby a tremendous sense of satisfaction. He was the Seven-Stud champ of the world. Inspired, he entered the no-limit Deuce-to-Seven Lowball event. And he won that. This time it was worth $90,000. Fortified by the satisfaction of having just claimed two world titles in vastly dissimilar forms of poker, he entered the Hold 'em grand championship with renewed optimism.

He finished seventh out of thirty-four entrants. No money, but again he'd made the final table.

"Next year . . ." said Doyle Brunson who had just claimed the second straight world championship for himself. "Next year you're going to be right in the running."

They were standing near the card room.

"Did you ask him yet?" It was Jack Binion's voice.

Both Bobby and Doyle pivoted to find the gregarious Binion smiling warmly.

"No, not yet," said Doyle.

"Ask me what?" Bobby demanded.

"Doyle's got a fabulous idea, but it's going to take you and a lot of other great players to pull it off."

The three of them went into the coffee shop to talk it over.

CHAPTER 23

A Labor of Love

"I'm writing a book," Doyle said.

"Good idea," said Bobby.

"Not just any book," said Jack.

"The ultimate book on poker," Doyle explained. "The bible."

"Good idea," Bobby said again, swallowing his coffee but burning his tongue in the process. "Damn! Hot!"

"Put some cream in it," Jack advised.

"I've got this writer Allan Goldberg whose gonna put it all together, brother. It'll be extremely detailed. Two, three hundred pages with card illustrations, mathematics and psychology. Instead of a general approach, we'll show them *exactly* what to do in every conceivable situation."

"Good idea. If you want to spend a couple months working on this thing. It'll take at least that long."

"No," Doyle argued. "Allan's going to put it all on tape and organize it. All we have to do is be interviewed and oversee the project. Besides, it's not going to be just me and you—"

"Hold it! How did I get dealt in?"

Doyle ignored Bobby and continued. "Not just me and you, but the best player in the world for every kind of poker as a collaborator. The best specialist. Like for high-low split, I want David Sklansky and for Lowball, Joey Hawthorne."

"And Chip Reese for Seven-Stud, and Mike Caro for Draw, right?"

"That's right, you must be reading my mind."

"And just how do you expect to get these people to devote any time to this?"

"Charm, Bobby. I'm going to use my charm."

♠

I mean, this was just the craziest idea I ever heard of. Doyle had dealt me in all right. I was his selection to collaborate on the limit Hold 'em section. That, in itself, was flattering, since I'd only recently polished my game to where I was happy with it. Here was Doyle "Texas Dolly" Brunson, the man who had won the last two world titles saying he considered me the best limit Hold 'em player in the world.

How his charm would work on those other superstars he wanted for collaborators, I had no way of knowing. But his charm had worked on me. Two days later I called him up and said, "Well, when do we start?"

Now, that was probably the dumbest thing I ever did.

"It will just take a few days," he told me. "About twenty hours of taped interview and then you can go back to your cherished life as a touring poker player." I've never heard him sound so effervescent. His optimism splashed over to me.

Then we got started. Well, I'll tell you, it didn't just take two days. I worked on it for a year solid, and so did Doyle and all the other collaborators.

I mean, we got obsessed with it. You just can't imagine . . . six grownup professional gamblers huddling sometimes till dawn to put strategies together. Giving away secrets. Consulting mathematicians. Refining and distilling until we were all so proud of the book we couldn't wait for it to hit the market.

And so it was a year later that we had this incredible argument in the offices of the company Doyle had started, called B & G Publishing.

"You can't sell it for a thousand dollars a copy, Doyle," I pleaded. "No one will buy it."

"Well, Bobby, when they hear what's in it—"

"Doyle, we all worked hard on this. We've got to find the price that will be most reasonable for sales."

"You saying it isn't worth a thousand dollars? We've put over six hundred pages into it. It took us a year. In fact, it took me longer than that. And I've got a half million dollars invested in it!"

"You'll end up selling only about five hundred of them, all to professional players."

"Well, I'd rather burn the book than sell it for less than five hundred dollars," said Doyle in one of his rare stubborn moods.

A week later, though, after talking it over with numerous advisers, Doyle phoned me up and said, "We're going to sell it for $100." He didn't sound too pleased about it.

But all I could say was, "Thank God!" I knew that the longest, toughest year of my life was not going to waste.

During that year, I did manage to spend two or three nights a week at poker. But instead of traveling, I played mostly in Las Vegas. It was a good year for Bobby Baldwin. So good that by the time the World Series of Poker came around again in May, 1978, I had my biggest bankroll ever. It grew to nearly $800,000. But three weeks before the tournament, I played a thirty-two hour session at the Dunes. It cost me $100,000, and when I drove away from the casino, I was feeling tired and irritable.

Suddenly there was this siren and a flashing light, and I had to pull over to the side of the road. The policeman came around to my window.

"Kind of a sloppy turn," he said.

I hadn't noticed, but he told me that I'd pulled out in front of a truck, forcing the driver to use his brakes. Then he asked for my driver's license.

"Oklahoma," observed the cop. "Live there?"

"Texas," I said, not thinking too clearly.

"Oklahoma license, Texas resident, Nevada plates," he mumbled. "Got a registration?"

I unlocked the glove compartment and handed him the document.

"This ain't you," he said.

"That's right, officer. This car belongs to Doyle Brunson. He's just letting me use it."

"Brunson, huh?"

"Right. You might have heard of him. Won the world poker championship two years in a row."

"Yeah. Big fellow, right, I seen it on the tube."

Suddenly I felt more at ease. Until he said, "Do you know a guy named Benjamin Forester."

"No. I don't think I ever heard of him. I meet a lot of people, so maybe I'd know him by sight. Why?"

"Just wondering. How is it you meet a lot of people you only know by sight? You an entertainer or something?"

"No, just a poker player."

"A poker player? You win?"

"Mostly. Not tonight."

"And you don't know a Benjamin Forester? Maybe someone you played poker with?"

"Maybe. But not someone I know very well. Who is he?"

"Lives here in Las Vegas," said the cop matter-of-factly. "Owns this car," he added.

I just slumped down in the seat, rested my elbow on the steering wheel and covered my head with my hands. The name Benjamin Forester swirled through my head like some evil code word. I felt a sweeping sense of doom.

"I want you to follow me to headquarters."

"Officer I don't mean to be disrespectful, but I'm just so tired. Could you call Doyle at his home, or even Jack Binion at the Horseshoe Club. They'll straighten it out."

"Poker, huh?" he murmured, giving me close scrutiny. Then he stepped back. He stood there for a long moment, sighed and shook his head. "Poker. Well, drive careful, here me?" And he returned to his squad car.

It seemed like a miracle. I drove away very, very carefully. I flopped onto my bed in near exhaustion, but before falling asleep, I phoned Doyle:

"Is Benjamin Forester a friend of yours?" I asked.

"Brother, he sure is. In fact he owns the car you were driving. "

"That so?" I said. "Well, I'll talk to you tomorrow, brother." I just flat hung up and slept forever.

The next few weeks, I concentrated on high-low split, a game I'd done a lot of homework on. I recovered what I'd lost the previous session and a little extra. By the time the World Series of Poker 1978 rolled around, I had my biggest bankroll to date—almost a million dollars—and, brother, I felt ready.

CHAPTER 24

High-Low Split*

COMMON MISTAKES

MISTAKE ONE:
Thinking of high-low split as an action game that offers an opportunity to play more pots

The truth is just the opposite. There are fewer profitable starting hands in high-low split than in Seven-Stud.

MISTAKE TWO:
Playing for the high end

This is a very serious error made by novices. A pair of kings is one of the worst possible starting hands, since it has only a fair chance of winning high and almost no chance of winning low. Most of the time, play for low and hope to luck into the high side.

---

* The assumption is that the game is *cards speak*. This means that the highest hand and the lowest hand split the pot, and there is no declaration. This was the most common form of high-low split played in public casinos at the time. A new form of the game, requiring eight-or-better to qualify for the low side of the pot, has since surpassed that form in popularity in casinos. However, cards speak is enjoying a resurgence.

MISTAKE THREE:
Playing all quality low hands aggressively

Some low hands are scarcely playable. Begin with 7 5 2 and you're asking for trouble, because you need a lot of help to compete for the high end, and your low chances are only slightly better than someone with 7 6 5.

MISTAKE FOUR:
Trying for half the pot

If you don't at least have an outside chance for the *whole* pot, don't commit your money.

MISTAKE FIVE:
Beginning with a face card

A hand like K 7 5 is almost always unplayable, even if suited. Even K A 2 of the same suit is marginal.

"Buried" hole cards... Up card showing...

High-low split: This starting hand is almost always unplayable.

MISTAKE SIX:
Continuing to play after catching a jack, queen or king on fourth street.

When you begin with a quality low hand and catch a paint on the fourth card, you should usually throw your hand away against a bet.

FINAL FORMULA

RULE ONE:

Don't play for the high side unless you're virtually assured of winning it and you're facing two or more opponents.

RULE TWO:

Your low starting hands should include an ace *or* have strong straight or flush potential.

RULE THREE:

Play hands that give you a shot at the whole pot.

RULE FOUR:

Seldom start with any hand that includes a face card.

RULE FIVE:

If you begin with a quality low hand and your fourth card is a paint, usually pass.

RULE SIX:

Don't generally begin with any pair other than aces, 5s, 6s, 7s or 8s—and only consider playing the smaller pairs if they're accompanied by a low rank.

RULE SEVEN:

Remember: If an opponent has two pair or three-of-a-kind, his lowest hand must—at best—include his *highest* card.

♠

The Horseshoe Club didn't have a year-round poker room. About two weeks before the first tournament, the Binion's move out some slot machines and bring in the poker tables. Having spent almost the entire year in Las Vegas working on Doyle's book, called Super/System, and also titled How I Made Over $1,000,000 Playing Poker, I was at the Horseshoe when the cardroom opened in April.

The poker players were so excited about the book's publication that a special booth had to be opened right in the casino just to handle the demand.

"You're Bobby Baldwin," a man said, coming up behind me. "Just read Doyle's book. I liked the way you two teamed up to handle Hold 'em. Never read anything like it. Didn't realize how poor I've been playing."

I turned around to discover the source of these words. He was a man of average size, immaculately dressed, pleasant and radiating a well-educated aura.

"How 'bout a little Hold 'em?" he asked. "No Limit. Maybe you, Doyle, me, and some of the other boys. I don't expect to beat you, but I'd enjoy the challenge."

We got to socializing in the coffee shop. Turned out his name was Chet Tower and he owned forty-seven laundromats and a couple of restaurants. I said I'd try to get the game together. Two hours later we were at a table consisting of me, Puggy Pearson, Doyle, and two other professionals.

Chet was so glad to meet Doyle that I thought the game would never get started. They just talked and talked. Poor Doyle had to answer about sixty questions. I remember wondering if I would be pestered to death if I were to win the world title. Oh, well, it was a downside I'd be proud to live with when the time came.

So, anyway, Chet just laid it on real thick about how he'd enjoyed the Hold 'em sections in the book. He said he'd just got his $100 copy yesterday and had already digested it. Naturally, Doyle and I were a bit skeptical, considering the average reader would have to spend a lot more time than that to handle the concepts. We started playing, and it became clear that Chet had not mastered as much of the game as he thought he had.

Finally I got involved in a large pot with this neophyte gambler. He brought it in for $800 and I called in the blind with just a 5 and a 3. It was the sort of hand I liked to stay for the flop with whenever he let me in cheaply. Any demonstration of loose play caused him to gamble recklessly.

The flop was king, 9, deuce: I checked, preparing to give up the hand now that nothing helpful had flopped.

He checked also. The next card was a 6. Except for the remote possibility of making an inside straight, my hand was hopeless. So I checked, again ready to fold should he make even a small wager. Again he checked. So we got the last card. The dealer turned it up slowly. A 4.

Well, now, I thought. This makes the picture a little different. Suddenly I had a straight. More than that, I had a lock on the pot, holding the best possible hand. I started debating how much to bet, but then I noticed the way his hand was subconsciously inching toward his stack. He was going to bet. I was positive!

"Check to you, Chet."

He didn't even hesitate. "I'll make a small wager. Say. . . oh. . . say about fifteen hundred." He pushed his bet neatly into the pot.

Well, I didn't hesitate long. I figured, if ever a man looked ready to call a disproportionately large bet, it was Chet Tower. I raised him $36,000.

He literally turned white. I've never seen anything like it. I was afraid he might be having a heart attack. His breathing was very labored

Well, he thought and thought. And thought. Then he slumped back to his chair in virtual resignation. For a moment I thought I'd lost the call.

Finally he said, "Bobby, I guess you've got me. But I can't see how I can throw this hand away . . ." He started counting through his chips. When he got finished, he slid them into the pot, calling my bet and leaving him only about twelve thousand in front of him.

He turned his hand over at the same time I did. 5 3! Well, I tell you, I've never played a weirder hand. I mean the guy had the absolute nuts. We both did. There was no possible way either of us could lose. But he had damn near folded, and finally, reluctantly he'd called. He hadn't even raised his last twelve thousand. Here was an intelligent, likeable guy who simply didn't understand Hold 'em.

Nobody said anything to embarrass the man, but later Doyle and I were alone in the parking lot and we laughed over it.

"I don't think he got around to reading the book yet," I speculated.

"Bobby, I <u>know</u> he didn't read it," Doyle agreed.

I entered the Seven–Stud tournament. This year it got to be just Doyle and me in the finals. I had to settle for second place, and that somehow sparked my competitive instincts. Something inside me got stubborn. This year everything felt right. When the big tournament came around next week, I'd be ready. Maybe I wouldn't win the world title. But I was sure going to give it one hell of a try.

BACKSTAGE

"How do you feel?"

"I'm not sure, Shirley. A little jittery inside, maybe. Does it show."

"No. You always seem unruffled to me." Shirley and Bobby kissed briefly and walked toward the door. They were in a hotel room upstairs at the Horseshoe, and it was only a short walk to the poker room. The no-limit Hold 'em tournament would begin in a few minutes, and there was no way he could delay making his appearance.

Shirley said, "Win it, Bobby. You've worked so hard. You deserve it."

"We both deserve it," he said.

In the hallway he slowed his pace, then came to a complete halt. They faced each other. As almost an afterthought, he told her, "This might sound silly, but everything feels right. Shirley, I think I'm going to win."

The CBS television cameras were already in place when they reached the card room.

It was an anticlimax. Doyle Brunson put himself all-in on two pair against a single pair of aces. Having the best of it isn't enough if your luck doesn't hold. Following the two-time world champion's premature ouster, other former world champs began to get eliminated. Amarillo Slim, Johnny Moss, Puggy Pearson. All gone.

When the first day of competition ended, the original field of forty-two had become thirty-one. Of those, Bobby had the second most money on the table, trailing Jay Heimowitz by less than $6,000. On the second day, the size of the ante and the blind increased from the previous session. And twice again during the day the antes and blinds grew in size. It's the policy with world championship poker tourneys that the size of the game builds inversely to the number of surviving players.

Bobby survived the second day, but had fallen to sixth. He had, however, added $10,000 more to his stacks during the grueling session.

Along the rail that separated the crowds of onlookers from the players, a magazine reporter asked Amarillo Slim, "By the way, you ever heard of this Bobby Baldwin kid?"

"Yep, sure have."

"Think he stands a chance?"

"I reckon he's gonna win," Slim said.

At the close of competition on the third day, the score was: Bobby Baldwin, $163,600, followed distantly by Crandall Addington, a congenial Texan. Only six contestants remained.

"I knew you could do it," said Shirley in the shelter of their hotel room.

"It's not over yet," Bobby reminded her.

It was and it wasn't. Fourth day play resumed at noon and by twenty till four that afternoon only Bobby and Crandall Addington were alive. Bobby held a $15,000 lead, but each man had over $200,000. The structure of the game became a $2,000 blind and a raise-blind of $4,000. That meant every pot had $6,000 in it, even before the cards were dealt.

It was cat and mouse. Cautious. You could read the intensity across Baldwin's face. There was even a slight expression of anxiety when his chips melted to a mere $142,500. At that point, Addington had almost twice that amount.

Hours passed quickly, and at eight o'clock the tournament director, Eric Drache, declared that the blinds would now be $3,000 and $6,000—by the time you received your cards, you were already staring at a $9,000 pot.

Bobby struck twice quickly and took the lead. Addington took this turn of fortune graciously. They kidded, they smiled, but Bobby's concentration was scrawled across his face. Even his posture belied his carefree patter. It was deadly serious to him. It had been a long, long road. Twisting, slippery, uncharted. And this is where it had brought him. The end was close now.

Addington went all-in and survived.

But the end came anyway. With Addington hanging on to a mere $42,000 against $378,000, Bobby made a $10,000 bet and got raised by what Addington had remaining. Even before the flop, both men showed their cards face-up on the table, and the CBS cameras focused on the hands. Two 9s for Crandall Addington, two queens for Bobby Baldwin.

The flop came queen, 9, king. Both men had three-of-a-kind, but now the only hope for Addington was to snatch the fourth 9. Even if the next two cards were a 10 *and* a jack, he would only split the pot. That latter possibility evaporated when fourth street turned out to be an ace. Now Bobby waited, a forty-three to one favorite to win the world championship on the next card. It was an easy calculation, breezing through his mind which he had trained to do problems vastly more difficult. Forty-three to one: forty-four cards remaining in the deck and only one that could keep Crandall Addington alive.

Only one... the 9 of spades.

Still he remembered other bad beats. In particular the game in Stillwater, Oklahoma splashed into his consciousness—the first time he'd ever played with a big-name professional. And Slim had watched him get drawn out on . . . two running 4s . . . seen him go busted and graciously try to hide his hurt.

"That's enough for me," he had said. And heading for his car and the lonely drive home to Tulsa, he had tried to smile convincingly.

But today wasn't Tulsa. Today the final card came: 10 of diamonds. The only losing card that could have quelled Bobby Baldwin's conquest remained cooperatively in the deck. This was one of the forty-three winning cards. And now it was over. He was the world champion of poker.

Bobby and Donna with George and Barbara Bush

CHAPTER 25

Unsorted Secrets

This section is intended to reiterate some of the concepts put forth in this book. Additionally, I'm including some odds and ends—advice I've collected over the years.

There are some things about poker in general that should seem obvious to anyone who takes the game seriously. One is that rudeness has no place in big-stakes poker. I just never knock anyone's play. There are basically two reasons. First, the weaker player does not want to be subject to ridicule and may decide to play a better brand of poker rather than suffer the insults. Second, when you make the game unpleasant for an opponent, he's likely to take his business elsewhere the next time. Still, I've seen professionals lose their temper and throw cards at weaker players. That's ridiculous. Just say, "Take the pot." And say it softly.

You should try to specialize in one or two forms of poker. But it pays— it pays heavily—to be an all-round card master. No one player can be the very best at every game. That's because there are those who devote almost all their poker time to specific games. Even so, you'll want your poker skills to be well rounded. You want to play what they spread, whether it's Five-Stud, Hold 'em, or high-low split. Never acquire a reputation for waiting to pounce on a game only when you're perfectly sure you have the best of it.

People generally enjoy a challenge. If you have an honest reputation, they'll play you because you're good. Don't hustle. Just yesterday I was in a pot with a man who said, "I know I shouldn't call this bet, but I want to beat the world champ!" Then he shoved $15,000 into the pot on a hand that didn't have a ghost of a chance.

Make your opponents feel they have a shot at a big win. If they feel you're apt to back off as soon as you take a small beat, they don't enjoy playing against you.

MIXING IT UP

Especially against strong opposition, it's important to frequently change the speed of your game. That means playing only the profitable hands for a long stretch, then blitzing the table with a rash of power plays and bluffs. Always change speeds suddenly. A gradual shift gives your opponents a chance to adapt, thus defeating your purpose—to catch them off guard.

In a no-limit game, making a large, aggressive bet is known as "taking a big position." I'm very reluctant to take a big position against unknown players. Before I commit a large share of my chips to any single pot, I want all the information on my opponent I can gather. For this reason, I tend to give newcomers more credit than they usually deserve. It's a strategy with the safety of my bankroll in mind. Occasionally those out-of-town pleasure players are considerably more sophisticated than they appear. Underestimating an opponent can be a devastating mistake.

Actually, poker strategy dictates that you play more aggressively against loose players. For some reason, this very obvious truth evades some serious poker students. You see them playing only the nuts and waiting for the loose players to hang themselves. Conversely, they try to overpower the rocks with fancy footwork until, eventually, they get snapped off. The reason they make this mistake is that there are elements of truth motivating their strategy. You can profit playing the nuts against a very loose opponent.

But you'll make much more by lessening your minimum playing requirements to accommodate the live one. And, yes, you can make a decent profit bluffing tight players at appropriate moments. But a game plan based on throwing large bets at them and raising whenever they enter a pot will sooner or later fail dismally. Remember, give action to action.

My belief is that, as a rule, conservative players can't beat no-limit poker.

BLUFFS

In general, weaker opponents who are playing primarily for entertainment are difficult to bluff. A player who is winning is apt to be more bluffable than usual. This is particularly true if the amount of the call would put him behind if he lost. Players who are losing are hard to bluff. They're apt to grab at straws in a desperate attempt to get even.

When there's a prearranged cutoff, or when the game is about to end for some other reason, bluffs are seldom profitable.

Nervousness is a good indication of whether an opponent is bluffing. "Obvious!" you say. Well, you'll be able to use this fact more profitably when you understand the reason for it. When a player has bet a strong hand, his only anxiety concerns: How big will the pot be? If he's bluffing, he's worrying: Will I win or lose? Now, the magnitude of those apprehensions isn't similar. The latter is of much greater concern to a player than the former.

Most players tend to be easily irritated while bluffing.

If you're playing against tight players, try to get them to agree to a proportionally large ante. With loose players, try for the opposite. Very conservative players tend to be uncomfortable with a large ante and play poorly. Loose players seldom adjust to ante size and play the same regardless. In a limit game, a professional always adjusts his minimum playing requirements to conform to the size of the ante. The bigger the ante relative to the bet size, the looser he plays.

BE COMFORTABLE

One of the biggest mistakes a player can make is to think of every pot on a win/lose basis. True, there are numerous hands that your skill can alter from defeat into victory just by the way you play your cards. But the really critical consideration, the thing that will weigh most heavily on your bankroll in the long run, is how much you earn on your winning hands and how much you limit the damage on your losing hands. The big victories are often getting an extra bet, saving a bet by not calling, and not playing an otherwise profitable hand because special reasons dictate a laydown.

Dress comfortably. There just isn't any way I can overstate this point. Do not attend a poker game formally attired. No ties, no scratchy material, no restricting tight clothing. You've got to be completely relaxed to focus on the hundreds of different interactions that make each poker hand different from the last one.

Of course, you'll want to steer your strategy so that most of your major confrontations are against weaker players.

Get sufficient sleep and don't play for too many hours.

Remember other players' habits, so that the next time you're in a game together, you'll know things about their playing mannerisms that they themselves are probably unaware of.

Concentrate even when you're not involved in a hand. Watch the players who are involved, and analyze their characteristics.

NAME PLAYERS

You always play to win. Winning is your motive. Never play for entertainment. Never play to gamble.

Occasionally, take vacations away from poker. Never play when you're emotionally upset.

If you should be in a game with a name player, study his habits closely. It will be a rare learning opportunity. If it's a world class player, give him the respect he deserves. But don't be intimidated by him. Just play your game the best way you know how.

Especially, don't try to impress a name player with elaborate maneuvers. I see many novices try to do this in a game against me. What they really want is praise.

They figure that they'll earn it if they pull off the nearly impossible. They might decide on some outrageous bluff against the loosest player in the game. Sooner or later they succeed, and they look to me for recognition. It doesn't seem to matter to them how many times they got caught bluffing previously or how much it cost them to make their little flash of glory.

Since some players have developed a degree of talent and want to impress me with their skills, I seldom give them any reinforcement. Being too lavish with, "That was the correct play," or "You analyzed that just perfectly," will cause a player to really take his game seriously. If he had any tendency at all to go on tilt and throw off money, he will no longer do it because he's playing solely to impress me. When I fail to give the reinforcement they're after, likely as not their play will become more and more bizarre in an effort to get it through my thick skull that I am, in fact, up against an accomplished player. That's when it's easy to make big money.

DESTRUCTIVE IMPULSES

Don't let your ego block your success. Play to win, not to bolster your ego. Don't plan to get back at someone who's just bluffed you out of a large pot. Let the law of probability take its course. If you never get even with the guy, you just never get even. So what? It's the amount of money you win during the year that really matters. That's how you keep score.

I've talked a lot about destructive impulses. The need to take chances, even reckless chances, is an inherent character trait of every successful gambler I've ever known. The difference between these winners and the would-be stars who bash themselves and their bankrolls into oblivion is this: Winners have stopped denying that these dangerous urges exist within them. They have come to terms with themselves. Once you're honest with yourself about your own nature, it's a lot easier to rationally map out a winning game plan and stick to it.

Craps and roulette don't mix with poker. To a poker player, gambling is science. Casino games are purely chance.

The ideal image at a poker table is honest and aggressive. Again, it's your reputation as a clean, honorable competitor that makes others want to gamble with you. This is doubly true if you're known as an action player. That's why I usually opt to put as much speed into a hand as possible. In the overwhelming majority of cases, when I have a choice between calling and raising, I raise.

There have been loners and bachelors who are superstars in the poker world. For me, though, a family life is very important. Ideally, your woman should be the kind who'll understand the volatile nature of gambling. She should be someone to confide in, good or bad. Be honest with her about how things are going.

RESPECT

I don't care what you've heard about supposed poker etiquette, it doesn't matter how friendly you are with the guy across the table or whether the fellow you're about to bet into saved your mother's life two years ago. <u>Never play anyone soft!</u> There may be rare times when you've got to keep from breaking up a game because that's your most profitable long-range objective. But profit should be the only thing that motivates your poker decisions. Period.

You don't want to call a weak opponent a "sucker." Likely as not, these casual players are highly skilled at some other profession. They're playing poker strictly for pleasure. And you should respect their right to do it.

When things don't go right, be a friendly loser, not a complainer. If you get caught bluffing, don't criticize the call.

Don't treat the money that you're winning with less respect than the money you came with. Sometimes you might find yourself thinking that, well, you didn't have this extra $15,000 when you sat down, so you might as well go ahead and take a few extra chances with it. Bad attitude. That money is just as much yours as the money you bought in with.

When you're stuck heavily in a game, try to win back a percentage of the loss. Stick to your original game plan, without taking suicidal risks in an attempt to get even.

MORE TIPS

Try to make weak and average players take a stand. Get them to put enough money in the pot so they feel they have a commitment to it. They'll seldom give up the hand at that point no matter how hopeless their subsequent calls seem.

People want to get into action, and consequently they're looking for reasons to call. In order for them to throw a hand away, the justification must seem overwhelming. Keep that in mind when playing against weaker opposition.

CHAPTER 26

On the Road Again

One of the primary functions of a traveling professional is public relations. You must respect the game enough to play honestly and mannerly. There is no excuse for poor manners in a private poker game. Socializing with big-money poker amateurs will increase the number of invitations you get. Golf, parties, dinners: these are all regular activities that I enjoy with wealthy pleasure players.

If you want to be invited to a game, say, "Bill, I was thinking of coming up your way next week. How's your game been?" Sort of feel it out. You don't want to pressure someone to invite you to a game where you're not really welcome. That just stirs up hard feelings and works against you down the road.

Be willing to help start games. That means playing in games that aren't particularly lucrative. Somebody's got to start them, and if you get the reputation for just waiting around until it looks juicy, you might find yourself uninvited next time.

Don't forget to honestly acknowledge that you're a professional card player. Don't say you're just in town visiting a friend. It might work once or twice, but the long run perspective is purely negative. Besides, I can't stress enough that people don't mind playing against strong talent so long as they aren't afraid of being cheated, so long as the game is pleasant, and so long as there's a chance for them to win big money in an action game.

From time to time, you'll intentionally take the worst of it. Maybe that means playing a game you're unfamiliar with against strong opposition. You've got to develop a reputation as an action player, willing to risk your money at anything. Naturally, you stick to whatever games you're best at.

PROTECTION

You should have a plan in case of a police raid or hijacking. Poker is pretty much a socially accepted activity in America. But some localities still fight hard to stamp it out as if it were a community menace. Check around before you enter a game and see if it's a safe city for poker. Think what you're going to do if you get raided. Usually, the only protection is to be courteous, and make certain to count the amount of chips you have in front of you. You and the other players should try to sort it out later. Police have the annoying habit of mixing all the chips and money together.

When someone comes crashing through the door, you're better off if it's the police. Hijackers are the more dangerous concern. They prey on private games, using everything from knives to machine guns. It isn't any fun. Try to escape according to a plan, using a rear entrance. If escape isn't possible, hide jewelry and some cash, but keep a few large bills so that the hijackers won't be angered. If it does turn out to be the police, tell them immediately that you have hidden some money and jewelry. Say exactly where. It goes in their reports and you'll likely be able to reclaim it at a later date.

Try to attend games where most transactions take place on paper. Credit games are much less likely to be robbed. Arrange for credit in advance whenever possible.

If you must carry cash, <u>don't flash money</u>. It's a good idea to keep your spending money and your bankroll in separate pockets.

Don't burn out a spot. As a traveling pro, I try never to take too much money out of a given game. It's just plain courtesy and common sense to move down the road before you wear out your welcome.

However, you shouldn't give up on a game because it hasn't been good for a few weeks. The tide changes. Weaker players come and go, and so do sophisticated players. Give the game a few more shots, and sometimes you'll be surprised at the change from one session to the next.

BANKROLL

Any great poker player that went broke probably didn't do it at a poker table. Keep control of your lifestyle in general. Don't overspend. Eliminate or at least limit your willingness to take bad gambles. Do you really know anything about thoroughbred horses, or are you just kidding yourself?

Bet enough so it hurts to lose, but not so much that you're concentrating on money and not poker.

Treat poker as a business.

Keep records. Don't kid yourself into thinking you're winning when you're not. If you're a traveling poker player, include your expenses in those records. Also, keep track of your traveling time.

Make sure you're emotionally capable of handling a lifestyle with vast fluctuations in day-to-day fortune. If it's security you're seeking, get a job.

CHAPTER 27

Whatever It Takes

JANUARY, 1979. Snow blankets everything. His front yard is a frozen, lifeless blend of white and night shadows. The phone rings.

"Jasper O'Connor's in a game at the Alamo Room," says a voice that Baldwin recognizes.

"Thanks, Shorty. I'll try to be there." He sighs, a mixture of excitement and frustration. It's after midnight and the Alamo Room is in Dallas. Still, millionaire Jasper O'Connor only plays cards two or three times a year, usually unloading between two hundred thousand and half a million. Bobby wants a piece of it.

"Shirley, I'm going to Dallas."

"Tonight? How will you get there? The highways are shut down just out of Tulsa. It was on the news. They're saying it's the worst blizzard since—"

"Would you hand me that phone book? Thanks."

Fifteen minutes later, Bobby has a private pilot on the line. *Dallas? Tonight? In this weather?*

"I'll pay whatever it takes. Can you do it?" *No. Not without a co-pilot and you couldn't find one this late at night. Probably tomorrow, though.*

"Well, don't go anywhere," Bobby urges. "I'll call you right back."

He dials another number. ". . . Hello, Al . . . well, this is Bobby, how you been? Sorry if I got you out of bed, but I need some help.

Did you say your brother-in-law has a commercial pilot's license? ... Yeah ... right ... What's his phone number?"

Five minutes later, Bobby rings the number he's circled in the yellow pages. "Okay, I got you a copilot. Let's go to Dallas."

The pilot turns out to be a rugged sort, and fully bearded. "These wings are frozen. All this ice ... There's no way we can take off," he explains to Bobby.

Al's brother-in-law arrives, his station wagon sliding into a snowdrift thirty feet beyond where he intended to park. He emerges wearing a ski mask. The three men merge. Great gusts of angry snow bite into their flesh. The agony of the wind obscures their voices and no one dares face into the blizzard. Their three cars are within twenty feet of the twin-engine aircraft.

"I was just telling Bobby," the pilot shouts to the newcomer, "we can't fly this bird out of here 'cause the wings are iced."

"Look!" says Bobby, a large chunk of ice held in his glove. "It comes off." And just to prove it, he struggles to liberate another sheet of ice from the wing. Finally a slab breaks free.

So, working two at a time and taking turns warming their hands against Bobby's car heater, the three men remove the ice within half an hour.

Only one engine starts. After several attempts, the second roars frigidly. It's two o'clock when they land in Dallas, two-thirty-six when Bobby strides into the Alamo Room.

He collides with a man rushing out the front door.

"Excuse me ... Oh, hi there, Bobby. I was just fiddling around playing poker and it got to be later than I thought. Got to rush to the airport. Chartered me a flight to Austin. See you around." He is extravagantly attired, all aglitter with diamonds and gold.

Politely, Bobby shakes the hand of Jasper O'Connor and says good-bye.

GREAT CARDOZA POKER BOOKS
ADD THESE TO YOUR LIBRARY - ORDER NOW!

WINNER'S GUIDE TO TEXAS HOLD' EM POKER by Ken Warren - The most comprehensive book on beating hold 'em shows serious players how to play every hand from every position with every type of flop. Learn the 14 categories of starting hands, the 10 most common Hold'em tells, how to evaluate a game for profit, value of deception, art of bluffing, 8 secrets to winning, starting hand categories, position, more! Bonus: Includes detailed analysis of the top 40 hands and the most complete chapter on hold'em odds in print. Over 50,000 copies in print. 224 pages, 5 1/2 x 8 1/2, paperback, $14.95.

KEN WARREN TEACHES TEXAS HOLD 'EM by Ken Warren - This is a step-by-step comprehensive manual for making money at hold 'em poker. 42 powerful chapters teach you one lesson at a time. Great practical advice and concepts with examples from actual games and how to apply them to your own play. Lessons include: Starting Cards, Playing Position, Raising, Check-raising, Tells, Game/Seat Selection, Dominated Hands, Odds, much more. This book is already a huge fan favorite and best-seller! 416 pgs. $26.95

WINNER'S GUIDE TO OMAHA POKER by Ken Warren - In a concise and easy-to-understand style, Warren shows beginning and intermediate Omaha players how to win from the first time they play. You'll learn the rules, betting and blind structure, why to play Omaha, the advantages of Omaha over Texas Hold'em, glossary, reading the board, basic strategies, Omaha high, Omaha hi-low split 8/better, how to play draws and made hands, evaluation of starting hands, counting outs, computing pot odds, the unique characteristics of split-pot games, the best and worst Omaha hands, how to play before the flop, how to play on the flop, how to play on the turn and river and much more. 224 pgs. $19.95

POKER WISDOM OF A CHAMPION by Doyle Brunson - Learn what it takes to be a great poker player by climbing inside the mind of poker's most famous champion. Fascinating anecdotes and adventures from Doyle's early career playing poker in roadhouses and with other great champions are interspersed with lessons one can learn from the champion who has made more money at poker than anyone else in the history of the game. Readers learn what makes a great player tick, how he approaches the game, and receive candid, powerful advice from the legend himself. The Mad Genius of poker, Mike Caro, says, "Brunson is the greatest poker player who ever lived . This book shows why." 192 pgs. $14.95.

BOBBY BALDWIN'S WINNING POKER SECRETS by Mike Caro with Bobby Baldwin. New edition—now back in print! This is the fascinating account of 1978 World Champion Bobby Baldwin's early career playing poker in roadhouses and against other poker legends and his meteoric rise to the championship. It is interspersed with important lessons on what makes a great player tick and how he approaches the game. Baldwin and Mike Caro, both of whom are co-authors of the classic Doyle Brunson's Super System, cover the common mistakes average players make at seven poker variations and the dynamic winning concepts they must employ to win. Endorsed by poker legends and superstars Doyle Brunson and Amarillo Slim. 208 pages, 5 1/2 x 8 1/2, paperback, $14.95.

POKER TOURNAMENT TIPS FROM THE PROS by Shane Smith - Essential advice from poker theorists, authors, and tournament winners on the best strategies for winning the big prizes at low-limit re-buy tournaments. Learn the best strategies for each of the four stages of play–opening, middle, late and final–how to avoid 26 potential traps, advice on re-buys, aggressive play, clock-watching, inside moves, top 20 tips for winning tournaments, more. Advice from McEvoy, Caro, Malmuth, Ciaffone, others. 160 pages, 5 1/2 x 8 1/2, $19.95.

HOW TO WIN AT OMAHA HIGH-LOW POKER by Mike Cappelletti - Clearly written strategies and powerful advice shows the essential winning strategies for beating the hottest new casino poker game—Omaha high-low poker! This money-making guide includes more than sixty hard-hitting sections on Omaha. Players learn the rules of play, best starting hands, strategies for the flop, turn, and river, how to read the board for both high and low, dangerous draws, and how to beat low-limit tournaments. Includes odds charts, glossary, low-limit tips, strategic ideas. 304 pgs, $19.95.

GREAT CARDOZA POKER BOOKS
ADD THESE TO YOUR LIBRARY - ORDER NOW!

NO-LIMIT TEXAS HOLD 'EM: The New Player's Guide to Winning Poker's Biggest Game by Brad Daugherty & Tom McEvoy. For experienced limit players who want to play no-limit or rookies who has never played before, two world champions give readers a crash course in how to join the elite ranks of million-dollar, no-limit hold'em tournament winners and cash game players. Readers learn the winning principles and four major skills: how to evaluate the strength of a hand, determine how much to bet, how to understand opponents' play, and how to bluff and when to do it. 74 game scenarios, two unique betting charts for tournament play and sections on essential principles and strategies, show you how to get to the winners' circle. Special section on beating online tournaments. 288 pages, $24.95.

BIG BOOK OF POKER by Ken Warren - This easy-to-read and oversized guide teaches you everything you need to know to win money at home poker, and in cardrooms, casinos and on the tournament circuit. Readers will learn how to bet, raise, and checkraise, bluff, semi-bluff, and how to take advantage of position and pot odds. Great sections on hold'em (plus, stud games, Omaha, draw games, and many more) and playing and winning poker on the internet. Packed with charts, diagrams, sidebars, and detailed, easy-to-read examples by best-selling poker expert Ken Warren, this wonderfully formatted book is one stop shopping for players ready to take on any form of poker for real money. Want to be a big player? Buy the Big Book of Poker! 320 oversized pgs, $19.95.

HOW TO BEAT LOW-LIMIT 7 CARD STUD POKER by Paul Kammen - Written for low-limit and first time players, you'll learn the different hands that can be played, the correct bets to make, and how to tailor strategies for maximum profits. Tons of information includes spread-limit and fixed-limit game, starting hands, 3rd-7th street strategy, overcards, psychology and much more. 192 pgs. $14.95.

OMAHA HI-LO POKER by Shane Smith - Learn essential winning strategies for beating Omaha high-low; the best starting hands, how to play the flop, turn, and river, how to read the board for both high and low, dangerous draws, and how to win low-limit tournaments. Smith shows the differences between Omaha high-low and hold'em strategies. Includes odds charts, glossary, low-limit tips, strategic ideas. 84 pages, 8 x 11, spiral bound, $17.95.

7-CARD STUD (THE COMPLETE COURSE IN WINNING AT MEDIUM & LOWER LIMITS) by Roy West - Learn the latest strategies for winning at $1-$4 spread-limit up to $10-$20 fixed-limit games. Covers starting hands, 3rd-7th street strategy for playing most hands, overcards, selective aggressiveness, reading hands, secrets of the pros, psychology, more in a 42 lesson informal format. Includes bonus chapter on 7-stud tournament strategy by World Champion Tom McEvoy. 160 pages, paperback, $24.95.

WINNING LOW LIMIT HOLD'EM by Lee Jones - This essential book on playing 1-4, 3-6, and 1-4-8-8 low limit hold'em is packed with insights on winning: pre-flop positional play; playing the flop in all positions with a pair, two pair, trips, overcards, draws, made and nothing hands; turn and river play; how to read the board; avoiding trash hands; using the check-raise; bluffing, stereotypes, much more. Includes quizzes with answers. Terrific book. 176 pages, 5 1/2 x 8 1/2, paperback, $19.95.

WINNING POKER FOR THE SERIOUS PLAYER by Edwin Silberstang - More than 100 actual examples and tons of advice on beating 7 Card Stud, Texas Hold 'Em, Draw Poker, Loball, High-Low and 10 other variations. Silberstang analyzes the essentials of being a great player; reading tells, analyzing tables, playing position, mastering the art of deception, creating fear at the table. Also, psychological tactics, when to play aggressive or slow play, or fold, expert plays, more. Colorful glossary included. 304 pages, 6 x 9, $16.95.

HOW TO PLAY WINNING POKER by Avery Cardoza - New and expanded edition shows playing and winning strategies for all major games: five & seven stud games, Omaha, draw poker, hold'em, and high-low, both for home and casino play. You'll learn 15 winning poker concepts, how to minimize losses and maximize profits, how to read opponents and gain the edge against their style, how to use use pot odds, tells, position, more. 160 pgs. $12.95

Order Toll-Free 1-800-577-WINS or use order form on page 207

THE CHAMPIONSHIP SERIES
POWERFUL BOOKS YOU <u>MUST</u> HAVE

CHAMPIONSHIP TOURNAMENT POKER by Tom McEvoy . New Cardoza Edition! Rated by pros as best book on tournaments ever written and enthusiastically endorsed by more than 5 world champions, this is the definitive guide to winning tournaments and a must for every player's library. McEvoy lets you in on the secrets he has used to win millions of dollars in tournaments and the insights he has learned competing against the best players in the world. Packed solid with winning strategies for all 11 games in the World Series of Poker, with extensive discussions of 7-card stud, limit hold'em, pot and no-limit hold'em, Omaha high-low, re-buy, half-half tournaments, satellites, strategies for each stage of tournaments. Tons of essential concepts and specific strategies jam-pack the book. Phil Hellmuth, 1989 WSOP champion says, [this] is the world's most definitive guide to winning poker tournaments. 416 pages, paperback, $29.95.

CHAMPIONSHIP TABLE (at the World Series of Poker) by Dana Smith, Ralph Wheeler, and Tom McEvoy. New Cardoza Edition! From 1970 when the champion was presented a silver cup, to the present when the champion was awarded more than $2 million, Championship Table celebrates three decades of poker greats who have competed to win poker's most coveted title. This book gives you the names and photographs of all the players who made the final table, pictures the last hand the champion played against the runner-up, how they played their cards, and how much they won. There is also features fascinating interviews and conversations with the champions and runners-up and interesting highlights from each Series. This is a fascinating and invaluable resource book for WSOP and gaming buffs. In some cases the champion himself wrote "how it happened," as did two-time champion Doyle Brunson when Stu Ungar caught a wheel in 1980 on the turn to deprive "Texas Dolly" of his third title. Includes tons of vintage photographs. 208 pages, paperback, $19.95.

CHAMPIONSHIP SATELLITE STRATEGY by Brad Dougherty & Tom McEvoy. In 2002 and 2003 satellite players won their way into the $10,000 WSOP buy-in and emerged as champions, winning more than $2 million each. You can too! You'll learn specific, proven strategies for winning almost any satellite. Learn the 10 ways to win a seat at the WSOP and other big tournaments, how to win limit hold'em and no-limit hold'em satellites, one-table satellites for big tournaments, and online satellites, plus how to play the final table of super satellites. McEvoy and Daugherty sincerely believe that if you practice these strategies, you can win your way into any tournament for a fraction of the buy-in. You'll learn how much to bet, how hard to pressure opponents, how to tell when an opponent is bluffing, how to play deceptively, and how to use your chips as weapons of destruction. Includes a special chapter on no-limit hold'em satellites! 256 pages. illustrated hands, photos, glossary. $24.95.

CHAMPIONSHIP PRACTICE HANDS by T. J. Cloutier & Tom McEvoy. Two tournament legends show you how to become a winning tournament player. Get inside their heads as they think they way through the correct strategy at 57 limit and no-limit practice hands. Cloutier & McEvoy show you how to use your skill and intuition to play strategic hands for maximum profit in real tournament scenarios and how 45 key hands were played by champions in turnaround situations at the WSOP. By sharing their analysis on how the winners and losers played key hands, you'll gain tremendous insights into how tournament poker is played at the highest levels. Learn how champions think and how they play major hands in strategic tournament situations, Cloutier and McEvoy believe that you will be able to win your share of the profits in today's tournaments -- and join them at the championship table far sooner than you ever imagined. 224 pages, illustrated with card pictures, $29.95

THE CHAMPIONSHIP SERIES
POWERFUL BOOKS YOU <u>MUST</u> HAVE

CHAMPIONSHIP HOLD'EM by T. J. Cloutier & Tom McEvoy. Hard-hitting hold'em the way it's played today in both limit cash games and tournaments. Get killer advice on how to win more money in rammin'-jammin' games, kill-pot, jackpot, shorthanded, and other types of cash games. You'll learn the thinking process before the flop, on the flop, on the turn, and at the river with specific suggestions for what to do when good or bad things happen plus 20 illustrated hands with play-by-play analyses. Specific advice for rocks in tight games, weaklings in loose games, experts in solid games, how hand values change in jackpot games, when you should fold, check, raise, reraise, check-raise, slowplay, bluff, and tournament strategies for small buy-in, big buy-in, rebuy, incremental add-on, satellite and big-field major tournaments. Wow! Easy-to-read and conversational, if you want to become a lifelong winner at limit hold'em, you need this book! 320 Pages, Illustrated, Photos. $39.95

CHAMPIONSHIP NO-LIMIT & POT-LIMIT HOLD'EM by T. J. Cloutier & Tom McEvoy
New Cardoza edition! This is the bible of winning pot-limit and no-limit hold'em tournaments, the definitive guide to winning at two of the world's most exciting poker games! Written by eight-time World Champion players T.J. Cloutier (1998 and 2002 Player of the Year) and Tom McEvoy (the foremost author on tournament strategy) who have won millions of dollars each playing no-limit and pot-limit hold'em in cash games and major tournaments around the world. You'll get all the answers here —no holds barred—to your most important questions: How do you get inside your opponents' heads and learn how to beat them at their own game? How can you tell how much to bet, raise, and reraise in no-limit hold'em? When can you bluff? How do you set up your opponents in pot-limit hold'em so that you can win a monster pot? What are the best strategies for winning no-limit and pot-limit tournaments, satellites, and supersatellites? Rock-solid and inspired advice from two of the most recognizable figures in poker — advice that you can bank on. If you want to become a future champion, you must have this book. 304 pages, paperback, photos. $29.95

CHAMPIONSHIP OMAHA (Omaha High-Low, Pot-limit Omaha, Limit High Omaha) by T. J. Cloutier & Tom McEvoy. Clearly-written strategies and powerful advice from Cloutier and McEvoy who have won four World Series of Poker titles in Omaha tournaments. Powerful advice shows you how to win at low-limit and high-stakes games, how to play against loose and tight opponents, and the differing strategies for rebuy and freezeout tournaments. Learn the best starting hands, when slowplaying a big hand is dangerous, what danglers are and why winners don't play them, why pot-limit Omaha is the only poker game where you sometimes fold the nuts on the flop and are correct in doing so and overall, how can you win a lot of money at Omaha! 230 pages, photos, illustrations, $39.95.

CHAMPIONSHIP STUD (Seven-Card Stud, Stud 8/or Better and Razz) by Dr. Max Stern, Linda Johnson, and Tom McEvoy. The authors, who have earned millions of dollars in major tournaments and cash games, eight World Series of Poker bracelets and hundreds of other titles in competition against the best players in the world show you the winning strategies for medium-limit side games as well as poker tournaments and a general tournament strategy that is applicable to any form of poker. Includes give-and-take conversations between the authors to give you more than one point of view on how to play poker. 200 pages, hand pictorials, photos. $29.95.

Order Toll-Free 1-800-577-WINS or use order form on page 207

POWERFUL POKER SIMULATIONS
A MUST FOR SERIOUS PLAYERS WITH A COMPUTER!
IBM compatibles CD ROM Win 95, 98, 2000, NT, ME, XP - Full Color Graphics

Play interactive poker against these incredible full color poker simulation programs - they're the absolute best method to improve game. Computer players act like real players. All games let you set the limits and rake, have fully programmable players, adjustable lineup, stat tracking, and Hand Analyzer for starting hands. Mlke Caro, the world's foremost poker theoretician says, "Amazing...A steal for under $500...get it, it's great." Includes free telephone support. New Feature! - "Smart advisor" gives expert advice for every play in every game!

1. TURBO TEXAS HOLD'EM FOR WINDOWS - $89.95 - Choose which players, how many, 2-10, you want to play, create loose/tight game, control check-raising, bluffing, position, sensitivity to pot odds, more! Also, instant replay, pop-up odds, Professional Advisor, keeps track of play statistics. Free bonus: Hold'em Hand Analyzer analyzes all 169 pocket hands in detail, their win rates under any conditions you set. Caro says this "hold'em software is the most powerful ever created." Great product!

2. TURBO SEVEN-CARD STUD FOR WINDOWS - $89.95 - Create any conditions of play; choose number of players (2-8), bet amounts, fixed or spread limit, bring-in method, tight/loose conditions, position, reaction to board, number of dead cards, stack deck to create special conditions, instant replay. Terrific stat reporting includes analysis of starting cards, 3-D bar charts, graphs. Play interactively, run high speed simulation to test strategies. Hand Analyzer analyzes starting hands in detail. Wow!

3. TURBO OMAHA HIGH-LOW SPLIT FOR WINDOWS - $89.95 -Specify any playing conditions; betting limits, number of raises, blind structures, button position, aggressiveness/passiveness of opponents, number of players (2-10), types of hands dealt, blinds, position, board reaction, specify flop, turn, river cards! Choose opponents, use provided point count or create your own. Statistical reporting, instant replay, pop-up odds, high speed simulation to test strategies, amazing Hand Analyzer, much more!

4. TURBO OMAHA HIGH FOR WINDOWS - $89.95 - Same features as above, but tailored for the Omaha High-only game. Caro says program is "an electrifying research tool...it can clearly be worth thousands of dollars to any serious player. A must for Omaha High players.

5. TURBO 7 STUD 8 OR BETTER - $89.95 - Brand new with all the features you expect from the Wilson Turbo products: the latest artificial intelligence, instant advice and exact odds, play versus 2-7 opponents, enhanced data charts that can be exported or printed, the ability to fold out of turn and immediately go to the next hand, ability to peek at opponents hand, optional warning mode that warns you if a play disagrees with the advisor, and automatic testing mode that can run up to 50 tests unattended. Challenge tough computer players who vary their styles for a truly great poker game.

---

6. TOURNAMENT TEXAS HOLD'EM - $59.95
Set-up for tournament practice and play, this realistic simulation pits you against celebrity look-alikes. Tons of options let you control tournament size with 10 to 300 entrants, select limits, ante, rake, blind structures, freezeouts, number of rebuys and competition level of opponents - average, tough, or toughest. Pop-up status report shows how you're doing vs. the competition. Save tournaments in progress to play again later. Additional feature allows you to quickly finish a folded hand and go on to the next.

DOYLE BRUNSON'S SUPER SYSTEM
A COURSE IN POKER POWER!
by World Champion Doyle Brunson

CONSIDERED BY PROS THE BEST POKER BOOK EVER WRITTEN
This is the classic book on every major no-limit game played today and is considered by the pros to be one of the best books ever written on poker! Jam-packed with advanced strategies, theories, tactics and money-making techniques - no serious poker player can afford to be without this essential book! Hardbound, and packed with 605 pages of hard-hitting information, this is truly a must-buy for aspiring pros. Includes 50 pages of the most precise poker statistics ever published!

CHAPTERS WRITTEN BY GAME'S SUPERSTARS
The best theorists and poker players in the world, Dave Sklansky, Mike Caro, Chip Reese, Bobby Baldwin and Doyle Brunson, a book by champions for aspiring pros - cover the essential strategies and advanced play in their respective specialties. Three world champions and two master theorists and players provide non-nonsense winning advice on making money at the tables.

LEARN WINNING STRATEGIES FOR THE MAJOR POKER GAMES
The important money games today are covered in depth by these poker superstars. You'll learn seven-card stud, draw poker, lowball, seven-card low stud (razz), high-low split (cards speak) and high-low declare; and the most popular game in the country today, hold'em (limit and no-limit). Each game is covered in detail with the important winning concepts and strategies clearly explained so that anyone can become a bigger money winner.

SERIOUS POKER PLAYERS MUST HAVE THIS BOOK
This is mandatory reading for aspiring poker pros, players planning to enter tournaments, players ready to play no-limit. Doyle Brunson's Super System is also ideal for average players seeking to move to higher stakes games for bigger wins and more challenges.

To order, send $29.95 by check or money order to Cardoza Publishing

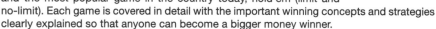

DOYLE BRUNSON'S SUPER SYSTEM - NOW JUST $29.95!
Yes! Please rush me Doyle Brunson's Super System - the 624-page masterpiece (now in paperback!) for serious poker players. Enclosed is a check or money order for $29.95 (plus postage and handling) made out to:

Cardoza Publishing, P.O. Box 1500, Cooper Station, New York, NY 10276

Call Toll-Free in U.S. & Canada, 1-800-577-WINS
or e-mail: cardozapub@aol.com

Include $7.00 postage/handling for U.S. orders; $17.00 for Canada/Mexico; HI/AK, other countries, $27.00. Outside U.S., money order payable in U.S. dollars on U.S. bank only.

NAME _____

ADDRESS _____

CITY _____ STATE _____ ZIP _____

MC/Visa/Amex Orders By Mail

MC/Visa/Amex# _____ Phone _____

Exp. Date _____ Signature _____

Order Today! 30 Day Money Back Guarantee!

Baldwin